Reinhold Niebuhr and Psychology

The Ambiguities of the Self

D1479043

MERCER
UNIVERSITY PRESS

Endowed by
TOM WATSON BROWN
and
THE WATSON-BROWN FOUNDATION, INC.

Reinhold Niebuhr and Psychology

The Ambiguities of the Self

Terry D. Cooper

MERCER UNIVERSITY PRESS

MUP/P388

Reinhold Niebuhr and Psychology
  The Ambiguities of the Self
Copyright ©2009
Mercer University Press, Macon GA
All rights reserved
Printed in the United States of America
First edition July 2009

The paper used in this publication meets the minimum requirements
of American National Standard for Information Sciences—
Permanence of Paper for Printed Library Materials,
ANSI Z39.48-1984.

Mercer University Press is a member of Green Press initiative
(greenpressinitiative.org), a nonprofit organization working
to help publishers and printers increase their use of recycled paper
and decrease their use of fiber derived from endangered forests.
This book is printed on recycled paper.

Library of Congress Cataloging-in-Publication Data

Cooper, Terry D.
    Reinhold Niebuhr and psychology : the ambiguities of the self /
Terry D. Cooper.
        p.   cm.
Includes bibliographical references and index.
ISBN-13: 978-0-88146-147-3 (pbk. : alk. paper)
ISBN-10: 0-88146-147-4 (pbk. : alk. paper)
    1. Niebuhr, Reinhold, 1892-1971. 2. Philosophical anthropology.
3. Psychology, Religious. I. Title.
BX4827.N5C66 2009
261.5'15092--dc22

                                                          2009004535

Contents

* * *

*For
Dr. James Armour
and the Armour Foundation,
with deep appreciation
for their encouragement and support.*

* * *

1

Why Niebuhr and Psychology?

*Man has always been his most vexing problem. How shall he think of himself?
Every affirmation which he may make about his stature, virtue, or place in the
cosmos becomes involved in contradictions when fully analyzed.*

—Reinhold Niebuhr

*Niebuhr was profoundly interested in both modern psychology and the social
sciences and is seldom given the credit he deserves for his critical and
appreciative appropriation of their insights.* —Don Browning

Reinhold Niebuhr and politics? Of course. Reinhold Niebuhr and social
ethics? Absolutely. But Reinhold Niebuhr and psychology? It may at first
seem to be a strange combination. Yet Niebuhr's analysis of the human condition inevitably led him into a dialogue with psychology. Further, his
theological anthropology, which many consider to be the most insightful in
the twentieth century, greatly contributes to a psychological understanding
of the human condition.[1]

Let me state this more directly. While Niebuhr was first and foremost
a theologian, social ethicist, and political thinker, these disciplines do not
"own" him. His thought has great relevance for psychology. Often writing
with blazing insight and analytical genius, Niebuhr was an avid student of
human nature. Further, Niebuhr frequently displayed a keen awareness of
the complexities and contradictions in his own psyche. Put simply, one does
not write with this level of penetrating insight and depth concerning the
human psyche without a sophisticated self-understanding. For this reason,
I believe Niebuhr was an astute observer of his own inner life, as well as a
highly informed commentator of our social existence. In fact, much of his

---

[1]Reinhold Niebuhr, *The Nature and Destiny of Man: A Christian Interpretation*, Gifford Lectures, 1 vol. ed. (New York: Charles Scribner's Sons, 1962, 1949:
1, 1941; 2, 1943); paperback repr. in 2 vols. with intro. by Robin W. Lovin
(Louisville: Westminster John Knox Press, 1996).

work bears striking similarities to his own mentors: Augustine, Luther, Pascal, and Kierkegaard.

Thus again, while Niebuhr will understandably be associated primarily with social ethics and political theory, his work is also a rich resource for psychology. Even though Niebuhr has little use for any theory of the self that does not also consider the realities of society and history, he also has little use for any social or political theory that does not understand the profound psychological dynamics of the self. Over and over again, Niebuhr resists any neat and tidy reductionism. As his biographer June Bingham has stated, "if one could fairly make an oversimplification of Niebuhr's thought, it would be that he is forever at war with oversimplification."[2]

Nevertheless, most psychologists have left Niebuhr alone. Even though Niebuhr mined the depths of Kierkegaardian anxiety, wrote interesting critiques of Freud and the neo-Freudians, and spent most of his entire career explicating the human condition, the value of his thought for psychology has often been missed. Even in the areas of pastoral counseling, one does not find an abundance of references to Niebuhr. Perhaps this is because Niebuhr is closely associated with social, ethical, and political dilemmas which seem removed from the personal struggles of the psyche. Also, perhaps Niebuhr's fast-paced style and keen eye for the world situation has communicated to some that he has little to say to the inner world of psychological experience. And further, Niebuhr has at times been quite critical of psychology. Yet as it turns out, many of those criticisms were later voiced by psychologists themselves. Self-indictments have been made against the discipline's tendency to think in asocial, apolitical, and ahistorical ways as it seeks to indulge the pleasures of inward expansion with little sense of communal involvement and responsibility.[3]

---

[2]June Bingham, *Courage to Change: An Introduction to the Life and Thought of Reinhold Niebuhr* (New York: Scribner's, 1961) 33.

[3]Christopher Lasch, *The Culture of Narcissism* (New York: W. W. Norton, 1978); Edwin Schur, *The Awareness Trap: Self-Absorption Instead of Social Change* (New York: McGraw-Hill, 1976); Martin Gross, *The Psychological Society* (New York: Simon & Schuster, 1978); Michael and Lise Wallach, *Psychology's Sanction for Selfishness* (San Francisco: W. H. Freeman, 1983); Robert Bellah et al., *Habits of the Heart: Individualism and Commitment in American Life* (Berkeley: University of California Press, 1985); Philip Cushman, *Constructing the Self, Constructing America: A Cultural History of Psychotherapy* (Cambridge MA:

Some experimental psychologists might well object that Niebuhr, while offering interesting speculations about human nature and history, is in fact merely an armchair philosopher and should not be taken seriously in the world of academic psychology. He steps outside the rigorous demands of a strictly empirical approach to psychology, an approach which considers only the evidence tediously accumulated from quantifiable methods. Indeed, Niebuhr makes no claims about neuroscience, biochemical processes, or the particular habits of laboratory rats. But neither do most theorists of personality. And even if one insists that the lab is the only appropriate standard for any discussion of the human condition, one has already moved beyond the lab to make such a statement. Even the most rigorous form of science cannot demonstrate that its limited methodology tells the entire story of the human condition. If the perspectives of Niebuhr, or anyone else for that matter, contradict the more limited but important specific findings of scientific psychology, then by all means, those theories need to be adjusted. But psychology does not usually remain strictly scientific in this narrow sense when it makes claims about human motivation, our basic human needs, the context of our lives, the standards of mental health and the good life, or what provides us with meaning and purpose. If we truly want to limit psychology to that which can be demonstrated in repeated laboratory experiments, then psychology will indeed become a much "thinner," if not anorexic, science. Plus, there is an entire underworld of positivist assumptions about the nature of reality buried beneath this "simple" empirical approach to the world. The switch from methodological naturalism to ontological naturalism is a very easy one to make. It is perfectly appropriate to narrow one's focus to carefully controlled data for the purposes of some psychological research. Yet these empirically strict and quantifiable methods hardly tell us all there is to know about the human psyche. And they certainly don't eliminate the fact that psychology, when dealing with the larger questions about human meaning, is an *interpretive* enterprise.

Faith, Reason, and Psychology

Once again, for the purposes of this study, the crucial level of dialogue between Niebuhr and psychology is at the level of philosophical anthropology. Niebuhr is not interested in overlooking laboratory experiments or

Perseus Publishing, 1995).

questioning the specific and concrete findings of empirical psychology. His interest is in the world view or background cluster of assumptions with which psychology does its work. His conviction is that psychology will be meaningless without these philosophical underpinnings, this larger conceptual context out of which it does its work. Thus, Niebuhr is interested in what Gadamer frequently calls the "horizon" out of which we do our theorizing.[4] While some psychologists may argue that their entire approach to the discipline is scientific and therefore void of this philosophical horizon, Niebuhr flatly denies it. We each bring presuppositions to our investigations, regardless of the extent to which we champion the Enlightenment goal of total objectivity. The idea of completely "emptying ourselves" of all our assumptions and presuppositions and approaching human existence strictly from the standpoint of neutral and objective reason is a modern fantasy which must be dismissed. To once again refer to Gadamer, we each bring to our theorizing an "effective history." By "effective history" Gadamer means a background of assumptions and conceptions which have already affected us before we even begin to officially theorize. Conceptually, no one emerges from a vacuum. If our current experiences have been shaped by past relationships, then surely our current ideas have been shaped by the traditions in which we have been immersed. Again, by the time we begin to formally conceptualize things, we have already been heavily influenced by the theories and assumptions of our cognitive landscape. We don't come to our theories empty-handed. Langdon Gilkey puts this sharply:

> Niebuhr was convinced that at the heart of any philosophy, however explicitly it might be based on scientific inquiry or rational speculation, lay its views on these human issues, on the questions of the meaning of life. For him each philosophy's understanding of fate and the tragic, of human evil and human renewal, shaped all of its other speculations about reality and knowing. For him, in other words, each philosophy has as its "hidden" foundation a particular "faith" in life's meaning, and hence its explicit philosophical reflections in fact manifest a religious substance and a religious criterion. In that sense for him every philosophy is comparable to any example of

---

[4]Hans-Georg Gadamer, *Truth and Method*, translation edited by Garrett Barden and John Cumming (New York: Crossroad, 1982, ©1975; *Wahrheit und Methode*, 1960) 2nd rev. ed., ed. Joel Weinsheimer and Donald G. Marshall (New York: Crossroad, 1990, ©1989).

theology.[5]

This is absolutely crucial to understand if we are to engage in a fruitful discussion between psychology and theology. Psychology is always based on key philosophical assumptions about the human condition—assumptions that deal with the ultimate context of our lives.[6] They tell us about what is humanly possible, how to achieve human flourishing, the sources which block that fulfillment, our primary ethical obligations, and the ultimate source of meaning and purpose underlying our activities. The fact that they might not explicitly announce these assumptions is beside the point; the important factor is that they exist and they guide the more modest claims of psychology. Let me state this as strongly as I can: While some may argue that a theologian such as Niebuhr is intruding on the turf of psychology and entering a conceptual world into which he does not belong, I would say the opposite, namely, that many forms of psychology, while pretending to be strictly scientific, have in fact entered onto Niebuhr's turf of ethics, philosophy, and even theology. Put another way, as psychology expands and elaborates on our lives, it loses its "strictly" scientific demeanor. But beyond that, even its more intensely empirical methods are based on philosophical assumptions which are up for discussion. Psychology can't have it both ways: Either it limits itself completely to strict empirical findings or it recognizes that it, too, is incurably interested in questions about the meaning, purpose, and direction of human life. It cannot engage in philosophical anthropology—which it inevitably does—and then hang out a "no trespassing" sign for those it deems "unscientific." Yet nevertheless, psychology sometimes wants to claim a scientific status while engaging in philosophical questions about human motivation, meaning, and the good life. For instance, it does its work with a huge assumption about what is and is not "healthy." That criteria for health will inevitably roll off the turf of a strict empiricism and onto the turf of philosophical anthropology. Niebuhr understood this as well as Tillich understood it.

Niebuhr also knew that finitude allows only approximations of truth

---

[5]Langdon B. Gilkey, *On Niebuhr: A Theological Study* (Chicago: University of Chicago Press, 2001) 21.

[6]For an elaboration of these fundamental, quasi-theological assumptions of psychology see Don S. Browning and Terry D. Cooper, *Religious Thought and the Modern Psychologies*, 2nd ed. (Minneapolis: Fortress Press, 2004).

rather than Absolute truth. In fact, few spoke more harshly against the dangers of thinking that one's historical, limited, and temporal thinking process has captured the final, definitive word on reality. As he put it so eloquently, "Each great thinker makes the same mistake, in turn, of imagining himself the final thinker."[7] Idolatry constantly tempts us to finalize and absolutize our own limited perspective. This deifies our viewpoint and often justifies a condescending attitude toward others. This is the *demonic* element within religion. We move from the conviction that we have experienced God to the notion that we perfectly represent God. While this encounter with the Divine would seem to prompt humility, that humility is often short-lived as we claim special privilege and identify our own self-interests with a Divine cause.

While Niebuhr fully grasped the historical and social location of all thought, however, he was not a radical relativist. If the elevation of our thinking to an ultimate status (idolatry) is one temptation, then a sense of meaningless is another. The end result of radical relativism—the conviction that all convictions have utterly equal value—is despair and a tendency to give up on life. This leads beyond skepticism to cynicism. If all opinions are of equal value, why think or struggle with life's ambiguities? Nothing matters anyway.

Niebuhr would therefore attack such radical postmodernists as Foucault or Lyotard for advancing a self-defeating philosophy. Niebuhr would agree that a completely "neutral" stance is an Enlightenment hope we must give up. He would further agree that foundationalism, the notion that we must build our thinking from an absolutely secure starting point, is also an impossibility. All thinking begins in faith assumptions, regardless of whether they are religious or secular. Yet being unable to offer *perfect* reasons or *absolute* reasons does not mean that we cannot offer *good* reasons. Foucault's extreme reading of Nietzsche pushes him toward such a self-sabotaging relativism that we might ask why we should take his claims as "better" than anyone else's. Foucault speaks powerfully against coercion as "terrorism" and calls for the denunciation of all oppressive systems. Yet Foucault's own philosophical underpinnings make it clear that there is no valid reason to say that liberation is superior to oppression. The result of the this sort of epistemology is skeptical silence, not argument. And yet Foucault makes plenty of arguments. Niebuhr would ask Foucault

---

[7]Niebuhr, *Nature and Destiny of Man* 1:195.

the same question he asked Marx, namely, why are you unwilling to turn your powerfully critical guns on yourself? Marx saw the corruptive ingredient of self-interest in all perspectives except his own and then believed that once the poor were liberated we can have utopia. Some radical forms of postmodernism are quite good at "interrogating" (one of their favorite terms) everyone but themselves. As theologian David Tracy puts it, "Any theorist is tempted to make her or his theory the one innocent, free noncontextual hope for emancipation and enlightenment."[8]

So again, while "complete objectivity" is not an option, Niebuhr would endorse what Paul Ricoeur calls "distanciation."[9] This is a moment within a conversation in which we attempt to distance ourselves from our own assumptions and examine them. While we will not be able to completely emancipate ourselves from our assumptions, we *can* look at them self-reflectively and critically. This is why Don Browning and I have argued for a *critical* hermeneutical approach to psychology.[10] This approach realizes that we each emerge out of faith traditions, but it doesn't end there. It argues that we can also critically reflect on those assumptions. Without this submoment of critical distanciation, intellectual conversation is not possible. We will simply be speaking past each other. Richard Bernstein states this point eloquently:

> For although all claims to truth are fallible and open to criticsm, they still require validation—validation that can be realized only through offering the best reasons and arguments that can be given in support of them—reasons and arguments that are themselves embedded in the practices that they have developed in the course of history. We never escape from the obligation of seeking to validate claims to truth through argumentation and opening ourselves to the criticism of others.[11]

Niebuhr's apologetics are built on the idea that *good* reasons can be

---

[8]David Tracy, *Plurality and Ambiguity: Hermeneutics, Religion, Hope* (San Francisco: Harper & Row, 1987) 80.

[9]Paul Ricoeur, *Hermeneutics and the Human Sciences: Essays on Language, Action, and Interpretation*, ed. and trans. John B. Thompson (New York: Cambridge University Press, 1981) esp. chap. 4.

[10]Browning and Cooper, *Religious Thought and the Modern Psychologies*, 2nd ed.

[11]Richard J. Bernstein, *Beyond Objectivism and Relativism: Science, Hermeneutics, and Praxis* (Philadelphia: University of Pennsylvania Press, 1983) 168.

offered for Christian perspectives. In a sense, he encouraged others to take Christian concepts out for a "test drive" and see if they explained human experience. For Niebuhr, a theology which does not enlighten human experience is worth very little.

Rationality and It's Limits

In Niebuhr's day, Christian theology was divided between its "kerygmatic" and "apologetic" poles. Today these categories have largely been replaced by the terms "postliberal" and "revisionist" theology. But the basic differences remain much the same. Kerygmatic or "proclamation" theology, perhaps best represented by Karl Barth, emphasizes the futility of trying to validate or justify the claims of faith before the bar of reason. It recognizes no common ground between God's revelatory message and human attempts to understand ultimate things. Our finitude limits us, but more than that, our sinfulness has a cognitive dimension. There can be no natural theology because all natural thought begins with humanity and tries to move upward toward the Divine. We can only know God when God reveals Godself. In other words, God must break through the confines of our finitude with a revelatory message. The heart of the kerygmatic approach is this: God's "Word" establishes its own verification and in no way depends on human cleverness or rational justification for its authenticity. Reason is useless in establishing this Divine truth; and even more, reason is useless in preparing for it. Human efforts play no role whatsoever in validating or authenticating this "Word" from a God who is "wholly other" than even our best attempts to grasp Divine matters. Reason is of course valuable in the service of faith. But this is a *redeemed* reason, a reason guided by faith. No one's faith journey begins as a result of his or her own reasoning powers.

In its extreme form, then, kerygmatic theology sees reason as utterly impotent when it comes to ultimate matters. Reason is not useful in seeing the *relevance* or *plausibility* of the Christian message. For Calvin, as well as for Barth, it is sheer folly to expect anyone to be converted to Christianity as a result of human persuasion. This is strictly the task of God's spirit. The minister's job is to remain loyal to the Christian proclamation and let God's "Word" authenticate itself. From the kerygmatic perspective, the attempt to defend this faith before the bar of natural reason is a waste of time. The message of the Gospel will never make sense to secular, fallen reason. Inevitably, say kerygmatic and postliberal theologians, the apologetic or revisionist theologian allows the standards of human rationality to control Divine revelation. Human cultural standards become the final arbiter of God's revelation. In short, apologetic theology rather pathetically seeks the approval of secular thought processes. It tries desperately to win the endorsement of fallen reason. It is afraid to allow the Gospel to speak for itself. Why put secular reason on such a pedestal? It is audacious to think that we need to do the work that only God's own spirit can do. Our intellectual maneuvers never lead anyone to faith. In fact, it is cognitive *hubris* to think it does.

Parallel to this extreme form of kergymatic theology is a heightened form of apologetic theology. This perspective argues that there is no substantial difference between God's revelation and what the human mind can uncover through diligent attentiveness to reason. Taking an extremely immanent view of God's presence in the world, it trusts the natural mind to eventually uncover Divine truth. Apologetic theology of this stripe argues that reason is the great friend and forerunner of faith. Our own natural inclinations toward ultimate things can be trusted. Sin has not so obscured Divine matters that we are unable to discover them. There is a smooth continuity between the ways of God and the ways of humanity. The evidence clearly points to the rationality, plausibility, and relevance of faith. And in extreme forms of rationalistic Christianity, our own cognitive abilities nearly become the instrument of our salvation.

Niebuhr can best be located between these two extremes. Like the kerygmatic and postliberal theologians, Niebuhr would argue that all theorizing ultimately begins in faith. This is the starting point of *all* thought, secular as well as religious. As Niebuhr puts it, "There is no vantage point, individual or collective, in human history from which we could judge its movements with complete impartiality."[12] If we did not approach the empirical world from the standpoint of interpretive assumptions, this world would make no sense. Again, no one can "prove" this starting point. We all reason within particular traditions and perspectives. Niebuhr would condemn as intellectual pride any apologetic attempt to *prove* the authenticity of faith. In fact, he argued that Jesus himself rejected signs and wonders as evidence for proving the tenets of faith.[13] A committed faith clearly extends

---

[12]Reinhold Niebuhr, *Discerning the Signs of the Times* (New York: Scribner's, 1946) 8.

[13]Reinhold Niebuhr, "Coherence, Incoherence, and Christian Faith," in *Christian Realism and Political Problems* (New York: Scribner's, 1953) 198.

beyond the bounds of what reason can accomplish. Further, Niebuhr would also agree with many kerygmatic theologians that sin—or what Niebuhr would term our excessive self-interest—always biases our "findings." Sin has cognitive consequences.

Yet Niebuhr would *not* agree with kergymatic theology concerning the *extent* of these cognitive consequences. While our attempts to seek God may be wounded and distorted, they are not destroyed. We still hunger for God, recognize our dependence on a force much larger than ourselves, feel a sense of unexplainable moral obligation, and long for forgiveness. These are natural capacities within every person. While reason may be limited, it is not utterly impotent as Barth proclaimed. Reason can be employed to see the inadequacies and limitations of alternative perspectives on the human condition. Reason can lead us toward a cluster of self-contradictions which need the assistance of a perspective greater than our natural reason. And as we have seen, reason is also useful in demonstrating the relevance of the Christian message. For Niebuhr, the Christian message directly addresses the deepest realities of our lives. Does this mean that reason can validate or demonstrate faith? Of course not. Does it mean that reason can be very helpful in leading one toward Christian commitment? Indeed. It is legitimate for faith to be *beyond* reason; but a healthy faith should never be *against* reason. If it is, then this opens the door to every possible irrational and absurd position which might come along. Thus Niebuhr does not think that natural reason is as antagonistic to faith as Barth believes. In fact, Christian faith need not be afraid of common human experience; instead, Christian faith greatly *illumines* and *clarifies* that experience. Gilkey puts this issue in a manner with which Niebuhr would agree:

> [W]hatever religious faith or theological expression we advance must be related to this worldly life, evident within it, and creative for it. The symbols of a relevant theology must explicate and illumine our ordinary existence in the world, and conversely, our experience of being in the world must give meaning and reality to our theological discourse.[14]

Niebuhr therefore believes that reason occupies a place in between St. Thomas Aquinas's elevation of it and Luther's denunciation of it. For Aquinas, Aristotelian rationalism can carry us far down the road toward an

---

[14]Langdon Gilkey, *Naming the Whirlwind: The Renewal of God-Language* (Indianapolis and New York: Bobbs-Merrill, 1969) 250-51.

understanding of God. Grace fulfills what natural reason has erected. Faith is an addition to reason and never a contradiction of it. Luther, on the other hand, with his strong belief in the devastating consequences of sin on reason, wanted to reject the cultural wisdom of this world, especially for the purposes of moving toward God. Liberal Protestant Christianity, of course, rejected Luther's pessimism, and tended to conflate reason and revelation. In other words, revelation tells us what our reason is already showing us. Revelation uses symbolic and picturesque language whereas reason makes this symbolism precise in its rational description. Philosophical theology "purifies" the poetic and symbolic world of the Bible and traditional faith. But while Niebuhr values the products of cultural wisdom, he also believes that *the most important aspect of cultural wisdom should be an awareness of its own limits*. A reasonable person recognizes that reason cannot solve all the mysteries of existence. Following Kant, Niebuhr argues that reason brings us directly into the brick wall of our own limitations. Again, the relevance of this for psychology is that we cannot ultimately explain ourselves. Niebuhr distances himself from any view which claims to have completely solved the riddle of human existence. A comprehensive view of ourselves must transcend our own rational investigation.

Stanley Hauerwas, a leading postliberal theological ethicist who, like Niebuhr, has also delivered the prestigious Gifford Lectures at Edinburgh, is quite critical of Niebuhr's apologetic approach. A follower of the kerygmatic tradition, Hauerwas flatly believes that Niebuhr has sold out the core of the Christian message in his attempt to be politically relevant. In fact, Niebuhr's problem is precisely the problem of most of mainline Christianity, namely, it tries desperately to win the approval and support of a secular audience as it translates its religious claims into secular categories. Christian apologists, argues Hauerwas, work very hard to make sure that secular philosophers, psychologists, and ethicists all come to the same conclusions that Christians come to. Their primary concern is to say, "See, we're all really saying the same thing." But once they have translated uniquely Christian notions into secularized categories, they are immediately met with the question as to why we need the "extra baggage" of theology. Secularists employ Occam's razor: Why hang onto an overly complicated explanation when a completely secular explanation will work just as well. As Hauerwas puts it, "The more theologians seek to find the means to translate theological convictions into terms acceptable to nonbelievers, the more they substantiate the view that theology has little of importance to say in the area of ethics."[15] For Hauerwas, Christianity, like all thought, is dependent on its historical community for its convictions and it will never be universally persuasive. This is a goal it should give up. It will never win universal secular approval, and what kind of Christianity would it be if it did? This so-called common ground is *not* available. Historical theologian Gary Dorrien summarizes Hauerwas's position:

> Christianity is not a perennial philosophy, a world-embracing universal faith, or even a particular system of beliefs. The center of Christianity is not a particular belief about Jesus constructed by the Church, nor is the purpose of Christian ethics to assume moral responsibility for organizing the world. The center of Christianity for Hauerwas is the community-forming way of Christ that inspires a new kind of corporate spiritual existence in an alien world.[16]

To state it as sharply as possible: Hauerwas believes that Niebuhr has ignored the theological foundations of Christianity and exploited Christian symbols for the purpose of developing a political theory. Hauerwas does not mince words:

> I think anyone who would put Niebuhr on the side of the angels must come to terms with the extraordinary "thinness" of his theology. Niebuhr's god is not a god capable of offering salvation in any material sense. Changed self-understanding or attitude is no substitute for the existence of a church capable of offering an alternative to the world.[17]

Niebuhr, on the other hand, would probably see Hauerwas's postliberal call for a community of faith radically distinct from public discourse as a form of sectarianism. It is not enough to simply proclaim the tradition and "let the chips fall where they may." We must be engaged with this world, and that will inevitably involve an apologetic task. Here, Reinhold was in tension with his brother, H. Richard, who in many ways was a precursor to the postliberalism advocated by Hauerwas. Richard Fox describes, rather accurately I think, how Niebuhr may have responded to Hauerwas's

---

[15]Stanley Hauerwas, "On Keeping Theological Ethics Theological," in *Revisions: Changing Perspectives in Moral Philosophy*, ed. Stanley Hauerwas and Alasdair MacIntyre (Notre Dame IN: University of Notre Dame Press, 1983) 31-32.

[16]Gary Dorrien, *Soul in Society: The Making and Renewal of Social Christianity* (Minneapolis: Fortress Press, 1995) 352-53.

[17]Stanley Hauerwas, *With the Grain of the Universe: The Church's Witness and Natural Theology* (Grand Rapids MI: Bravos Press, 2001) 31.

postliberalism.

> From Reinhold's standpoint, his brother's perspective was too resigned, too passive, too ready to abandon the world to its sins. He would probably have had equal difficulty accepting the theology of postliberals. Their stance would have struck him as insufficiently secular, too churchy, to timid about using the world's methods to reshape the world. He would have bemoaned its refusal to absorb and rekindle the secular liberal agenda. For him postliberal theology would have amounted to a withdrawal from public concerns, a privatization of faith.[18]

The question of how hard the theologian should work in making the Christian message tenable to an unbelieving world has been with Christianity since its first encounter with Greek philosophy. Niebuhr, perhaps because of personal temperament as well as theological conviction, could have never be content working underneath a faith umbrella that did not engage the secular world around him.

Niebuhr as Neoliberal

We have seen that Niebuhr does not fall into the extreme corners of a kerygmatic or apologetic approach. While rightly labeled as more of an apologetic than a kerygmatic theologian, he does *not* believe, as did much of nineteenth- and early twentieth-century Protestant liberalism, that reason and human aspirations clearly open the door to faith. Certainly to those Protestant liberals who heard Niebuhr's thundering voice in the early 1930s, he was not one of them! Yet neither was Niebuhr comfortable within conservative circles. He had surely digested a heavy dose of the historical-critical approach to the Bible and had little use for any claims of biblical inerrancy. He clearly distanced himself from a literalistic and historical interpretation of the Bible. He embraced what he understood as the "permanent myths" or eternal stories of the Bible. While he chastised Rudolf Bultmann for wanting to eliminate *both* primitive *and* permanent myths, he clearly read the Bible symbolically. When pushed to its literal meaning, Niebuhr tended to describe it with one of his favorite words, "absurd."

While Hauerwas and others are right when they claim that Niebuhr remained more committed to theological liberalism than his frequent title

---

[18]Richard Wightman Fox, "Niebuhr's World and Ours," in *Reinhold Niebuhr Today*, ed. Richard John Neuhaus (Grand Rapids MI: Eerdmans, 1989) 13.

of "neoorthodox" suggests, Niebuhr nevertheless attacked two core assumptions of theological liberalism. The first was the assumption of historical progress, the idea that humanity is evolving morally as well as biologically. This notion of social progress was buried deeply within the soil of the latter nineteenth century. The assumption was largely taken for granted. Unlike the twentieth century, the nineteenth century did not have jolting evidence which shattered this bold confidence. And the second optimistic assumption was akin to the first, namely, that human nature is basically good. Evil is an external problem, a problem which civilization will eventually be able to eradicate. The notion of personal sin was therefore largely a hangover of the middle ages and reformation.

Niebuhr relentlessly attacked both of these assumptions. Again, while he was profoundly interested in social issues and held a disdain for privatistic piety, he utterly resisted any notion that our primary problem is external to our own freedom. Poverty is bad, but it does not *cause* sin; oppression is dehumanizing but it is not the direct *cause* of sin; racism is surely horrible, but it is not the master explanation for all of sin; and sexism is deplorable, but it cannot account for all sin. While Niebuhr remained very attentive to social and systemic injustice, he refused to believe, as did Marx, that once things were divided fairly we would have no "sin" problem. For Niebuhr that was simply naïve. We need not look at the world or our own natures through rose-colored glasses. We need instead a realistic assessment. And somewhat ironically, Niebuhr suggested that a sober and realistic assessment of human nature will keep us from the fall into cynicism brought on by the collapse of our inflated view of human potential. In other words, the exaggerated claims about human goodness "set us up" for a brutal fall once we get a comprehensive view of ourselves. Put simply, most cynics were once exaggerated optimists. After human nature has been knocked off of its pristine pedestal, many become quite despairing.

Niebuhr once stated, "I have carried on a warfare with Christians who think they can solve everything by love."[19] Niebuhr came to his Detroit pastorate with the liberal conviction that love is the solution to every moral problem. Yet the move from Yale to Detroit brought with it a great deal of cognitive dissonance. His belief in human potential and historical progress became more and more shaky as he watched an industrial city without

[19]Quoted in June Bigham, *The Courage to Change: An Introduction to the Life and Thought of Reinhold Niebuhr* (New York: Scribner's, 1961) 15.

unions, child labor laws, welfare programs, and unemployment compensation exploit and oppress people. This disjunction between classical liberalism and his actual life experience brought on a crisis in Niebuhr's understanding of the human condition. Put simply, his Detroit experience did *not* match his Yale world view. Human beings did not seem nearly as polite, moral, or "good" as he had hoped they were. Gradually, Niebuhr became suspicious of any view which suggests that we can easily shed our excessive self-regard as we sacrificially focus on others. His prior optimism appeared to him as more and more naïve. He came to believe that part of the problem with nineteenth-century theological literalism was its belief that the ethical demands of Jesus could be immediately applied to larger social and political realities. The ultimate demands of the love commandment and the proximate demands of a social ethic were not one and the same. We cannot use the ideal of *agape*, or complete self-sacrificial love, as a standard for social justice. While *agape* does not take into consideration the issue of mutuality and the calculation of rights, any realistic social ethic must take these into consideration. The Gospel of Matthew, for Niebuhr, was driven in part by an ideological motive to prove that Jesus was a more rigorous law giver than Moses. Nineteenth-century liberalism found in the ethical teachings a standard for social transformation. Correspondingly, it argued that Jesus was himself a moral optimist, a great believer in human potential. It was Paul, and not Jesus, who corrupted this optimism and offered a pessimistic and dark understanding of human nature. As an optimist, Jesus simply told people what was right and expected them to do it. He set the precedent, according to the social gospelers, of using love as the ultimate standard for all of life, including social and political conflicts. For Niebuhr, this "love solution" was naïve and dangerous.

Jesus' teaching was important as an ideal, but not as a genuine possibility within historical existence. For instance, the command to not be anxious about our lives, our bodies, or the future is an important goal for which to strive, but is existentially impossible. Our very condition as a mixture of finitude and spirit places us in an anxious situation. Ideally, we can trust God and thus our anxiety will not become corrupted by egoistic preoccupations about security. This faith in God could cancel out the destructive consequences of anxiety. But no one, in fact, can maintain this. Ideally, a trust in the providence of God could hypothetically lead to a lack of concern about shelter and food, as well as a disregard for social approval and possessions. Yet this ongoing, abiding trust in our ultimate Source, particu-

larly given the vulnerabilities and insecurities we face daily, is not a
realistic hope.

But Niebuhr's point was not to portray human beings in the most
negative light he could. He repeatedly stated that the gloomy picture of
human nature in the Reformers was excessive and tended to eradicate any
positive elements in humanity. Niebuhr was no fan of self-hatred. Perhaps
the reason he gained somewhat of a reputation as a sin-obsessed thinker in
the early twentieth century was precisely because he believed that human
optimism was so widespread that it needed to be challenged. Without a
crisis of faith in our own omnipotence, we would never understand our need
for God. Once again, for Niebuhr the human intellect must bump into its
own limitations before it will see the relevance of faith. Believing that
reason can usher in a perfect world is surely an obstacle to dependence on
God as the ultimate Source of our strength. As Niebuhr put it, "Religion is
the hope that grows out of despair. It is the ultimate optimism which
follows in the wake of a thorough pessimism."[20]

Balancing Individual and Social Concerns

As I previously mentioned, Niebuhr believed that any view of the world
which did not consider humanity's social and historical existence is always
short-sighted. While he shared a great affinity for Kierkegaard with the
European existentialists, at least according to Gilkey, Niebuhr was never as
"individualistic" as many European neoorthodox thinkers were.[21] For
instance, while Niebuhr was heavily influenced by Brunner's *Man in
Revolt*, he seemed to bring individual awareness into the larger stream of
historical consciousness and social existence.[22] The plight of the individual
and the direction of history were incurably intertwined. Niebuhr would have
certainly agreed with Christopher Lasch's criticism in *The Culture of
Narcissism* that the second half of the twentieth century led to an excessive
focus on the self which lacked a historical continuity with the past.[23]

---

[20]Reinhold Niebuhr, *The Contribution of Religion to Social Work* (New York:
Columbia University Press, 1932) 73.

[21]Langdon Gilkey, *On Niebuhr: A Theological Study* (Chicago: University of
Chicago Press, 2001) 20.

[22]Emil Brunner, *Man in Revolt: A Christian Anthropology*, trans. Olive Wyon
(London: Lutterworth, 1939; orig. *Der Mensch in widerspruch*, 1937).

[23]Christopher Lasch, *The Culture of Narcissism* (New York: W. W. Norton,

Private, personal concerns which ignore a larger picture of the world were for Niebuhr very unattractive. This is also true of Niebuhr's lifelong disdain for any form of personal piety which overlooks the crucial issues of social justice. Whether the source is pop psychology or pop religion, Niebuhr rejects privatistic and socially indifferent faith.

Niebuhr's nuanced commentary on humanity's social existence, however, should not obscure his insight into the inner dynamics of the human condition. As Robin Lovin suggests,

> Niebuhr's assessment of social realities was also guided by attention to the psychological forces at work. Here, he was less influenced by theory than by his insights. Anxiety about the insecurity of our position in the world and guilt about the things we have done to achieve and hold it lad us to fashion images of our own vulnerability and purity and provide powerful incentives to believe in what we have made. The ideals and values to which social classes have and political interests groups appeal to justify their claims are thus more than ideological smokescreens to conceal their real economic interests. They also defend against the threats posed by our own anxiety, and they protect our illusions form the reality of ourselves and our past.[24]

Niebuhr, then, is an interesting mixture of individual and social emphases. Gilkey is clearly right that Niebuhr explores the human being in history rather than merely searching through the human psyche. And Niebuhr is profoundly interested in issues of social justice and political concerns. In fact, perhaps no theologian has focused more ferociously on the social implications of excessive self-interest. Yet Niebuhr utterly refuses to blame the problem of human destructiveness or sin on social and political processes which "impose" themselves from without. He is constantly aware of the manner in which *individuals* mishandle their freedom in the face of anxiety. He radically departs from any suggestion that cleaning up the social environment will eliminate evil. The social and historical location of evil makes no sense without a certain readiness or inclination within the human heart. Thus for Niebuhr, the *ultimate* location or source of sin is not in oppressive systems, a lack of education, or any form of inequality. The ultimate source of sin is internal. Even if we eliminate the distortions in our

---

1978).

[24]Robin W. Lovin, *Reinhold Niebuhr and Christian Realism* (New York: Cambridge University Press, 1995) 7-8.

social world today, we still have the problem of ontological anxiety—a problem which will inevitably, but not necessarily, lead to distortions tomorrow. If anything characterizes the thought of Niebuhr it is this deep belief that sin cannot be reduced to sociopolitical causes.

Again, this makes Niebuhr a most interesting thinker: On the one hand, he profoundly dislikes any brand of psychology which does not consider the social and historical location of the individual; on the other hand, he retains a strong personal emphasis on sin and refuses to reduce the source of sin to outside factors. Thus, while Niebuhr would agree with many of the social critiques of psychology's tendency to be self-absorbed, he would disagree that any external explanation of human destructiveness is tenable. Here we see a twofold disagreement with Marx: (a) Niebuhr departed with Marx's utopian conviction that all social conflict can eventually be eliminated when the oppressed are liberated, and (b) Niebuhr did *not* believe that the ultimate source of all alienation is economic. However much Niebuhr digested Marx's critique of social pretensions, he had also digested a thoroughgoing Kierkegaardian understanding of the role of anxiety and the personal misuse of freedom in sin. I believe this double focus in Niebuhr, a focus which sustained a creative tension in his thought, is especially relevant for today's world. How easily the pendulum swings from an exaggerated individualism to a sociopolitical reductionism of the self. One view decontextualizes the human psyche to the point that he or she is no longer a sociohistorical citizen; the other extreme loses a sense of personhood as it reduces the inner world to a social and political construction.

This Niebuhrian balance is especially important in contemporary pastoral theology. Moving away from an earlier preoccupation with psychology and a near equation of salvation with self-realization, some pastoral theologians are swinging to the opposite perspective of antipsychological, prosociological liberationist thought. This move can be very helpful *if* it is held in tension with a careful attentiveness to the inner life. But the repentance from psychology has nearly turned into a conviction that there is a social, political, or economic cause for all that ails us. One reductionism is replaced by another. Niebuhr can help us maintain a dual focus. We are failing people if we attempt to turn their socioeconomic problems into merely intrapsychic struggles. Yet we are also failing people when they bring their intensely personal struggles to us and all we can do is call our local politician. Put another way, the need for psychotherapy will not go away just because we better understand public policy. If excessive "psychologizing"of pastoral care has been a danger in the past, surely excessive "politicizing" of pastoral care is a danger today, especially in many mainline Protestant groups. Selfhood is sometimes completely reduced to a sociopolitical construction.

June Bingham, whom I have previously mentioned as one of Niebuhr's friends and biographers, makes the following interesting observation about Niebuhr's view of the self:

> Niebuhr is far more patient with people who deny the existence of God than with people who deny the existence of an integral self. These people, whether sociologists or psychologists, economists, or political scientists, are guilty, in Niebuhr's eyes, of a serious mutilation of reality.[25]

Again, while Niebuhr is very interested in the sociopolitical dimensions of human life, he profoundly rejects any notion which suggests that the self is nothing more than a sociopolitical production. This would obviously put Niebuhr in deep variance with some dimensions of postmodern thought which deconstruct the notion of the self and argue that it is completely constructed.

Niebuhr's Primary Focus: Human Nature

It is my conviction that the interest in the philosophy of human nature, which seemed to underlie *all* of Niebuhr's writings, is precisely what brings him into the greatest dialogue with psychologists. As Peter Homans has stated, "Niebuhr has made the problem of the nature of man central to his many and otherwise extremely diverse interests and concerns."[26] As a master of comparative views of human nature, Niebuhr pushes psychologists to expose their root assumptions about the human condition. Beneath his magnificent and sometimes sweeping characterization of an entire period of thought is an eagerness to reveal the primary assumptions about human nature. His deep interest in intellectual history often zeroes in on the philosophy of the human. While Tillich, who was much more explicitly involved in discussions with psychology and psychotherapy, is often credited with pressing psychology toward its philosophical premises, Niebuhr, too, regularly engaged in his own form of pushing social scientists

---

[25]June Bingham, *Courage to Change* (New York: Scribner's Sons, 1961) 89.
[26]Peter Homans, *Theology after Freud* (Indianapolis: Bobbs-Merrill, 1970) 23.

toward a more philosophical discussion.[27] As Gilkey suggests, Niebuhr always went "straight for their doctrine of human nature."[28] Every philosophical approach has a hidden cluster of assumptions about human potential and possibilities, the source of human destructiveness, what restores "fallen" humanity, and what is the ultimate reality in which we have "faith." No matter how scientific or secular a viewpoint may claim to be, it always has faith in something, even if it is the individual or collective rationality of science. All competitive perspectives have assumptions about what heals us individually, socially, and historically. Each perspective has views about the nature and power of human reason, the significance of the human will, the issue of conscience, the problem of guilt, and the role of self-interest in daily life. In short, this is the realm of psychology.

The Self as Both "Revealed" and Studied

For Niebuhr, one of psychology's most dangerous errors is to assume that a knowledge of oneself is no different than the knowledge of an object in the natural world. In agreement with Augustine, Niebuhr frequently asserts that we can never know ourselves "within ourselves." As Peter Homans puts it, "Niebuhr insists that with regard to the most fundamental recesses of the self, it is finally known from 'beyond' itself." The self can, in and of itself, know its world and to some extent its own internality; but its knowledge of its essential nature is grounded in a fundamental or special experience which it cannot of itself create. This does not eliminate the significance and importance of psychology. Yet psychology, as a finite, human enterprise, cannot tell us the ultimate truth about ourselves, at least not if it stays within the confines of a scientific discipline. While psychology can greatly contribute to our self-knowledge, there is another form of "knowing" which is beyond the scope of strict psychological investigation. This involves a dramatic encounter with a source of meaning beyond ordinary reason and empirical methods. Put simply, the essential self is *revealed* rather than scientifically discovered. This "ultimate" story of our lives connects the human mystery with the Divine. Thus, Niebuhr follows Calvin's lead in declaring that in the final analysis it is impossible to have a complete psychology without a theological understanding of the

---

[27]Terry D. Cooper, *Paul Tillich and Psychology* (Macon GA: Mercer University Press, 2006).

[28]Gilkey, *On Niebuhr*, 21.

relationship between humanity and its Source. Perhaps this can be stated even more directly: *We are ultimately dependent upon God for a full self-understanding.* The final purpose, direction, and meaning of human life cannot be separated from its grounding in God.

As we have seen, some psychologists may immediately object that their discipline has no business speculating on this ultimate context of human experience. Psychology has no time for such armchair theorizing. It is, after all, a science. Yet two responses can be made to this claim. First, if psychology does indeed maintain a humble empirical stance, it can tell us some important things about proximate causes and small areas of verifiable data. This is important and it can be used to check and challenge larger claims about the human condition, claims which may contradict these scientific findings. In such a situation, these larger claims must be adjusted. Yet as I have already indicated, very few psychologists stay committed to a humble form of empiricism. Instead, following Comte, they move toward a more grandiose empiricism which claims to bear the only truth, the final truth, and the only meaningful way of describing the human condition. This epistemology obviously goes beyond what empirical methods can uncover. Again, it moves from a naturalistic method to a naturalistic ontology. Because its method can only investigate certain areas of human experience, then those areas are all there is! A narrow methodology easily leads to a narrow world view. Nothing outside of a strict empiricism is even worth discussing. If our methods cannot verify it, it must not be real. We find here a definite assumption about the ultimate context of human experience. A "humble" method becomes a dogmatic world view. Of course empirical psychology must assume a naturalistic methodology or psychology could never be considered a science. But a naturalistic method does not have to imply a naturalistic ontology in which empirical verifiability becomes the final word on *all* truth. Science, when it is functioning as science, must bracket metaempirical issues. Put simply, it has no comment. Yet invariably we see scientists such as Richard Dawkins move beyond this scientific framework and make metaphysical claims while pretending to operate within a strictly scientific method.[29]

The "smaller" questions of psychology inevitably lead to the larger questions about human being. All psychology eventually becomes

---

[29]Richard Dawkins, *The God Delusion* (Boston: Hougton Mifflin, 2006).

philosophy, or as Don Browning and I have argued, even quasi-religion.[30] Metaphysical assumptions lie beneath even our most "practical" behavior. Without these assumptions, human life would be suspended and frozen.

But Niebuhr is not a fideist. He does not simply say that the deeper truths about ourselves are revealed and that we must not put them to any sort of rational test. While these beliefs about the human condition go beyond reason and empirical investigation, they do not contradict either. Otherwise we would simply be embracing nonsense. A paradox is not a contraction, and a belief about the human condition which can be scientifically falsified must be abandoned. But Niebuhr's empiricism is much broader than what can be demonstrated in a psychological laboratory. Life itself is Niebuhr's lab. He invites us to compare our assumptions about the human condition with individual, social, and historical existence. Does it adequately account for the reality we encounter? Does it offer a comprehensive explanation of life as we observe it. Human experience, in Niebuhr's view, can confirm or falsify our basic beliefs. He invites us to put them to the test. This is Niebuhr's confidence: What may at first seem like the "absurd" claims of revealed truth can actually account for the ambiguities of human experience. In fact, for Niebuhr, a biblical account of our lives, when taken symbolically rather than literally, offers greater comprehensiveness than its secular rivals.

Thus, while Niebuhr's view of the ultimate context of human life begins in faith, it doesn't stay there. It is a faith which seeks meaning, a faith which is not afraid to allow its assumptions to be compared with the assumptions of others. Niebuhr is not a foundationalist who argues that he can cognitively start from scratch and rationally convince us of us starting principles. He knows that all thought begins with faith in something. Yet, he is quite ready to offer arguments as to how his "faith" is consistent with human life as we know it. We may not be able to offer final, definitive, and utterly convincing reasons for our faith. Yet we can offer reasons which demonstrate that our faith is certainly relevant to the world as we experience it. Gilkey puts Niebuhr's apologetic in clear perspective:

> This is the heart of his apologetic: he does not prove this vertical dimension or the relatedness to God which it implies. Rather he seeks to persuade us that we cannot make either human nature or history intelligible without that dimension,

---

[30]Browning and Cooper, *Religious Thought and the Modern Psychologies*.

that other viewpoints contradict either themselves or the facts, and that a biblical understanding rightly interprets the common but otherwise incoherent facts of experience.[31]

Also, as we have seen, the Christian message will seem more plausible if the Christian theologian does his or her job of revealing the ultimate inadequacies of other perspectives. In this sense, Niebuhr is a "theologian of the cross." By this I mean that our self-reliant cognitive efforts must be broken as a necessary step to accepting the Christian message. Our intellectual efforts are like all human efforts—they can never deliver us from our predicament. Intellectually arriving at the ultimate truth about ourselves with our own limited resources is simply another form of intellectual Pelagianism, or self-salvation. Our minds, as well as our wills, need grace.

The Horizon of Psychology

In his insightful study of Niebuhr in 2001, Gilkey stated that no one, to his knowledge, had tried to present Niebuhr's well-known political and ethical views in the light of Niebuhr's *entire theological viewpoint*.[32] While some have appreciatively read Niebuhr's political and ethical perspectives only to disconnect them from his overarching theology, Gilkey believes that everything Niebuhr had to say about social and historical existence is ultimately grounded in his theology. As Gilkey puts it, Niebhuhr "understood politics and ethics theologically, in relation to what he regarded as the Christian understanding of human being, of the creativity and ambiguity of freedom, and of the course of history under God."[33] Some, however, wanted to embrace the political teachings of Niebuhr while ignoring his theological beliefs. As Robin Lovin puts it, "Political thinkers admired Reinhold Niebuhr's insights into the fundamental importance of power in democratic politics or his warnings to America to take its own virtues too seriously, but many thought that these insights could stand on their own, without the theological dynamics to which they were linked in Niebuhr's mind. They have

[31]Gilkey, *On Niebuhr*, 80.
[32]Gilkey, *On Niebuhr*, xiii.
[33]Gilkey, *On Niebuhr*, xiii.

been called 'atheists for Niebuhr'."[34]

In a manner similar to Gilkey's thesis, I will argue throughout this book that the theological horizon is always a part of Niebuhr's social-scientific thinking, and hence, important for his understanding of psychology. Yet as I have already indicated, I believe that such a horizon exists behind every theory of psychology. Niebuhr's sometimes biting and insightful analysis of human existence is part of a larger framework which understands the ambiguities of life as part of a disrupted relationship with our creative Source, God. This "vertical" dimension becomes central in understanding Niebuhr's horizontal analysis. Put simply, social injustice and human destructiveness are intimately connected to our idolatrous attempts to replace God. This God replacement, as we shall see, was for Niebuhr a very subtle process rather than a conscious and deliberate denouncement of the Divine. It is ultimately a product of the same form of self-deception which psychologists, and especially psychoanalysts, have pointed out.

So as I attempt to mine Niebuhr's insights for a discussion with psychological theory, I am aware that his psychological wisdom cannot and should not be extracted from his larger theological framework. I have no intension of doing this. But, as we have seen, Niebuhr himself was extremely interested in demonstrating the relevance of his theology through empirical validation. Niebuhr routinely invites his readers to see if his conclusion fit the "facts" of everyday life. In this approach Niebuhr was heavily influenced by William James and American pragmatism. From his student days at Yale until the end of his life, Niebuhr was far more interested in demonstrating the relevance of the Christian message than in pondering its ontological underpinnings. In this sense, of course, he differed greatly from his friend and mentor, Paul Tillich.

Yet in spite of some areas of disagreement, one of the great unifiers of Niebuhr and Tillich was their deep conviction that life is thoroughly ambiguous. This may at first seem trite but it is a very important point. Creativity and change are always accompanied by tragedy, violence, and strife. There is no form of evolutionary progress which will carry us beyond this human predicament. Perhaps the most difficult task is to look at the world realistically without becoming cynical. Yes, human beings are wonderfully creative but they are also hazardously destructive; they are

---

[34]Robin Lovin, *Reinhold Niebuhr and Christian Realism* (Cambridge UK: Cambridge University Press, 1995) 33-34.

capable of a noble interest in the welfare of others but they are often excessively self-concerned. Niebuhr hammered away at any perspective which did not take into consideration both the heights and lows of the human condition. We are clearly a mixture of high aspiration and destructive self-preoccupation. Niebuhr believed that there is a saint in every sinner and a sinner in every saint. Either/or thinking about the human condition completely distorts a realistic picture of who we are. However hard we may try, we will never be *more* than human or *less* than human. Regardless of how spiritual may be our appearance, we each struggle with issues of excessive self-regard; and regardless of how lowly or "animalistic" may be our appearance, we still carry the capacity for a spiritual self-transcendence. We cannot escape this condition. No amount of asceticism will get rid of our natural appetites; and no amount of animal activity will get rid of our spiritual dimension. They are completely interlocked. This is one of the reasons that Niebuhr so resented any form of religious life which claimed an immunity to the struggles of "natural" existence. Like a bullet out of a chamber, Niebuhr would target various forms of spiritual pride. And for Niebuhr, this moral and spiritual pride, as we shall later see, was much more poisonous than the more "obvious" forms of sin. No matter what we do with our "spirit" we cannot eliminate our bodies; and no matter what we do with our bodies we cannot eliminate our "spirit." This juxtaposition of nature and spirit in every living person creates anxiety, which is the breeding ground of excessive self-regard. It is to this important theme in Niebuhr's thought that I now turn.

2

Anxiety and Excessive Self-Regard

Anxiety, as a permanent concomitant of freedom, is thus both the source of creativity and a temptation to sin. . . . The two are inextricably bound together by reason of man being anxious both to realize his unlimited possibilities and to overcome and to hide the dependent and contingent character of his existence. —Reinhold Niebuhr

For Niebuhr, it is absolutely essential to understand the nature and dynamics of anxiety if we are to grasp the human condition. Like his friend and colleague Paul Tillich, Niebuhr separated neurotic or psychologically caused anxiety from ontological anxiety, an anxiety which is simply built into the very structure of life. Thus what are now commonly referred to as the anxiety disorders (phobias, generalized anxiety disorder, panic disorder, posttraumatic and acute stress disorder, obsessive-compulsive disorder) are not primarily what Niebuhr had in mind when he used the term "anxiety." These neurotic forms of anxiety are amendable to psychotherapeutic treatment. Ontological anxiety, on the other hand, is the condition of *all* human life. We are anxious because we see both our limits and our limitless possibilities. Such is the condition of creatures who stand at the juxtaposition of nature and spirit. Both death and freedom scare us. Gilkey states this well:

> We are vulnerable, insecure, and mortal creatures, in constant peril. As self-transcendent, we feel and in fact see this situation and are anxious. And since our self-transcendence and the imagination that springs from it are unlimited, there are no possible limits to our anxiety about our security in either space or time. If we control our own valley, we can picture a new enemy on each neighboring hill—and every succeeding hill. If we have sufficient food for the present winter, we can imagine now our hunger in the next year—and every subsequent year. Our anxiety—hence our will to power and our greed and hence again our imperialism against every potential neighbor—is unlimited.[1]

---

[1]Gilkey, *On Niebuhr*, 104.

Anxiety is built into the human situation, a part of our essential structure. It is therefore not synonymous with sin. If anxiety equaled sin, then humans would not be responsible. Instead, anxiety, as the existentialists have pointed out so well, is the breeding ground for enormous creativity as well as destructiveness. Anxiety is an important force in human productivity, a necessary part of all fruitful labor. But anxiety can easily push us toward an attempt to establish a form of security which is not humanly possible. Our search for truth can become a dogmatic clinging to a particular perspective as the final authority; our desire for intimacy can push us toward a frantic and smothering control of another; our wish for economic comfort can drive us into an idolatrous preoccupation with wealth; our urge for stability can push us into a lust to possess everything around us. In short, whatever its form, destructive anxiety always drives us toward an attempt to be more-than-human. We try to "outsmart" our finitude. It is, in short, an attempt to be God. Security is turned from a finite good to an infinite god. We believe that we must provide our own final form of self-assurance, yet this is something we were never meant to do. And no matter how hard we attempt to achieve this security, we know at some level that it is based on a delusion. Thus, our attempt to escape anxiety *creates more anxiety*. Like a person in quicksand, we struggle relentlessly, yet we know, at least at some level, that we are still going under. In fact, as Tillich was fond of pointing out, the refusal to accept our ontological anxiety is what perpetuates neurotic anxiety.[2] Thus, it is not insecurity *per se* which is our problem; it is instead our attempt to hide or cover up that insecurity which leads to an even greater, spiritual insecurity. This is what Niebuhr meant when he said, "sin compounds the insecurity of nature with a fresh insecurity of spirit."[3] Thus, as Stephen Evans puts it, "while anxiety is not inherently pathological, it has taken on a pathological character in sinful creatures. The connections therapists have discovered between anxiety and pathology are genuine."[4]

Anxiety about our limitations, then, has led to a prideful self-assertion

---

[2]Paul Tillich, *The Courage to Be* (New Haven CT: Yale University Press, 1952) esp. chaps. 2 and 3.

[3]Niebuhr, *Nature and Destiny of Man* 1:207.

[4]C. Stephen Evans, *Soren Kierkegaard's Christian Psychology* (Grand Rapids MI: Zondervan, 1990) 64.

in defiance of those limitations. Anxiety about our limitless freedom, on the other hand, leads to a self-avoidance in which we back away from the frightening world of human possibilities. One response to anxiety inflates the self; the other response avoids the self.

Thus for Niebuhr there is a direct connection between anxiety and the claims for infinite certainty in life. Anxiety pushes us toward exaggerated and inflated notions that we somehow possess absolute knowledge. Having risen above the fray of finitude, we now "own" the final Truth once and for all. Our intellectual anxiety hides behind our intellectual pretension. Again, rather than acknowledging our *natural* anxiety, we often try to hide it and thereby create an even greater *spiritual* anxiety. Niebuhr states it as follows:

> If the fault is spiritual and not natural, then a spiritual resolution is required at the deepest level; not mere education, more inquiry, more intelligence, excellent as each of these may be. Rather we need the religious recognition or our own involvement in pride, humble repentance about our claims for security, for truth, and for virtue, and finally the acceptance of forgiveness and the beginning of trust. There is, hence, in Niebuhr a final transcendence of humanism, even the best humanism, into the necessity of the vertical dimension inherent in human being.[5]

Thus, in trying to eliminate an inevitable anxiety of nature we create an unnecessary anxiety of spirit.

Thomas Oden, in one of his earlier works, *The Structure of Awareness*, describes, in good Niebuhrian fashion, how we unwittingly intensify our struggles with anxiety by elevating finite and limited *goods* to the status of *gods*.[6] Any good in life can become a god *once we make it pivotal for our very existence*. A college education, a good job, economic security, or the joys of traveling are all "goods". However, we can turn each of these goods into gods by making them something we worship, something we can't live without, something of *ultimate* significance for us. This process of idolatry creates further anxiety because any of these things could be taken away from us at any moment. The loss of a "good" may be very sad and disappointing; but the loss of a "god" can be utterly devastating. And the anticipation of losing a god brings on destructive, rather than creative, forms of anxiety. So by elevating goods to the status of gods, we intensify our

---

[5]Gilkey, *On Niebuhr*, 107.
[6]Thomas C. Oden, *The Structure of Awareness* (Nashville: Abingdon, 1969).

anxiety.

Distrust and Anxiety

For Niebuhr, there is an intimate connection between our distrust of God and our level of anxiety. Two things are particularly important to remember about Niebuhr's discussion concerning this distrust in our Source: (a) he obviously draws language from human experience and uses it analogously to describe our relationship with God, and (b) he is not describing a single, conscious act of distrust and defiance which occurs at a specific time. It is not as if any of us can scan our histories and recognize a particular moment in which we chose to distrust God, act rebelliously, or turn our own finite existence into the center of the universe. Throughout Western history there has been a temptation to turn our "sinful inclinations" into a singular, conscious act of perversity. Many have read back into history or individual awareness a specific time of violating our relationship with God. But if we examine our own lives, at what point did we make this break? At what moment did we fall into estrangement as a result of our own self-centeredness? How "old" were we when all this happened? Most of us would have to say that it is impossible to locate a specific time and place in our personal history, just as it is impossible to pinpoint a specific time and place in our collective human history. To impose upon our estrangement a deliberate, completely conscious moment is ridiculous. Instead, the experience of estrangement seems to capture every moment of our experience. It is a "fall" from our potential to our actual self. Trying to locate a specific preestranged period of our developmental histories will prove unsatisfactory. Instead, the fall describes the here and now. At some level we each know that we "should be" better than we are. This is not always neurotic perfectionism or an abusive superego. It is instead the calm and sober realization that we fall short of our best intentions. It is not something for which we need to berate ourselves or feel inordinate shame. Instead, it is a full recognition of our human condition.

It is at this point that Niebuhr would strongly disagree with much of contemporary pop-psychology's position that we simply have a wrong perception of ourselves. Some popular psychologies suggest that our primary problem is that we have learned to think negatively about ourselves and this negative thinking, rather than any sort of actual inadequacy, is the main problem. Our brokenness is an illusion and we must simply learn to conceive of ourselves in a different manner. We have somehow erroneously picked up the crazy message that we are flawed and even "sinful." What we must do is clean up this self-perception and refuse to think this way about ourselves. We must muster up the cognitive strength to reverse this way of thinking and to realize that our so-called inadequacies are an illusion. All forms of self-condemnation and guilt, therefore, are based on a radical misperception of who we are. We must learn to combat this unrealistic way of thinking and learn to muffle an uneasy conscience.

Niebuhr would respond to this perspective by insisting that it will not help us to repress our own sense of falling short, no matter how much we invest in a new image of ourselves. Again, at some level, we know better. This certainly does not mean that we should spiral into an excessive, toxic shame which views the self as unredeemable. That, ironically, becomes an inverted sense of arrogance as we think we are "beyond" forgiveness, a position which surely exaggerates our own dark side. The point is to accept our own shortcomings with a humble desire to change. However much we may protest it, most of us are garden-variety human beings, at least where sin and grace is concerned. We are all too similar to others. What is needed is an honest self-estimate that neither exaggerates our greatness nor our wretchedness. We are neither saint nor worm.

The Limits of Cognitive Therapy

Psychotherapeutic attempts to "think our way out of our estrangement problem," for Niebuhr, as for Tillich, fail to realize that our reason, too, is affected by our anxious self-concern. Cognitive therapists such as Aaron Beck and Albert Ellis ultimately believe that through unbiased, unruffled rational thinking, we can end our neurosis and even deal with the so-called existential anxieties of life.[7] This assumes that reason can operate above the world of ontological anxiety and insecurity. Beck, in fact, flatly denies existential anxiety, arguing instead that there are cognitively distorted fears behind our *angst*.[8] It is possible for reason to ultimately smoke out all these fears, name them, and cognitively "conquer" them. For Niebuhr, this trust

---

[7]For a theological critique of Ellis and Beck, see Browning and Cooper, *Religious Thought and the Modern Psychologies*, 2nd ed., chap. 10. For a critique of Beck's cognitive approach to hatred, see my *Dimensions of Evil: Contemporary Perspectives* (Minneapolis: Fortress, 2007) chap. 4.

[8]Aaron Beck and Gary Emery with Ruth L. Greenberg, *Anxiety Disorders and Phobias: A Cognitive Perspective* (New York: Basic Books, 1985) chap. 1.

in a godlike reason which can step outside our of our existential condition and calm the waters of ontological anxiety is most unrealistic. Niebuhr would quickly ask, "Who is capable of such a perfectly unbiased, neutral, and nonanxious cerebral process?" This is a form of cognitive pride which ultimately denies our own finitude and props up reason as the ultimate Source of all salvation. It is the epitome of the Enlightenment in personal, psychotherapeutic form. It makes audacious claims to have found a means of self-rescue within a finite realm. It claims an immunity from exaggerated self-interest, an immunity that does not exist apart from a trust in the creative Ground of existence. Cognitive therapy can be wonderfully helpful in dealing with the everyday neurotic problems which emerge in our lives. But when it claims to tame even the existential anxiety and despair associated with being a finite, self-aware creature, it has clearly overstepped its bounds. Niebuhr was not a basher of the effectiveness of psychotherapy, *provided that psychotherapy did not make claims far beyond its reach.* Put another way, psychotherapy can help us clear the runway of neurotic pathologies in order to deal with the larger questions of life, purpose, and value. But psychotherapy cannot "fix" the ultimate riddle of human existence. If it attempts to do so, it is functioning as a religion and not merely as a method of psychological healing. As Browning and I have argued, there is nothing wrong with psychotherapy entering the larger discussions of which religion has been a part.[9] But when it does so, it should quit claiming to speak from a strictly "scientific" viewpoint and realize that it, too, is offering metaphysical and at least quasi-theological commentary.

Niebuhr, then, frequently pointed his critical guns at humanity's self-healing powers and found those resources wanting. His assumption, similar to Luther's, was that an analysis of human resources for handing our ultimate dilemma will lead to a necessary despair. This collapse of our idolatries, or beliefs in our own salvific methods, is a necessary step toward a transcendent hope. This is not to say that we should not make gallant attempts to solve all the problems we can. Surely Niebuhr was a major problem solver. But his conviction is that the human attempt to solve our deepest, spiritual dilemmas will prove unsatisfactory. Why? Because it makes the colossal assumption that our lives depend only and totally on *us*. We supply our own ultimate meanings and purposes. We do this by

---

[9]Browning and Cooper, *Religious Thought and the Modern Psychologies*, 2nd. ed.

replacing God as the Source and Center of our own lives. Our faith, then, is in our own efforts. Denying a need for an ultimate Source to strengthen us, we become the captains of our own ships and therefore define ourselves as the center of Reality. It is the belief in our own strategies, our own reason, and our own will power which will provide the ultimate meaning of our existence. We have no need for a relationship with our Creator. We can paint a cosmic picture that has no need for God as our Source.

The Many Faces of Pride

It is this process of radical self-dependence and denial of a need for the Transcendent which is the backbone of Niebuhr's understanding of pride. Obviously, while the word "pride" may occasionally be used in a positive manner ("She takes pride in her work") Niebuhr used it only in a very negative way. This pride, as we have seen, is intricately tied to distrust. Out of a distrust in God, we turn to our own resources to solve the riddles of our existence. While Niebuhr focused primarily on pride's puffed up qualities, pride does not always appear "puffed up." In fact, it may not seem arrogant or full of itself at all. It may take a more quiet and seemingly modest form of simply relying on one's own strategies to eliminate the problem of life's anxiety or insecurity. It may even attempt to resolve anxiety by turning someone else into one's god. In other words, it may attempt to escape the existential anxieties of this world by drowning oneself in the life of another. It may avoid selfhood by obsessing on something or someone else. Nevertheless, for Niebuhr, this is pride. Why? *Because it always involves an attempt to settle our ontological dilemmas through our own efforts.* It still involves an excessive preoccupation with self-security. An element of insecure self-absorption is still present. Thus, whether our idolatry is self-aggrandizement, the worship of another, or a frantic and self-defeating attempt to dodge our own inner life, the result, for Niebuhr, is a form of pride. Thus, pride is a *theological* problem even when it does not appear to be a *psychological* problem. This point is crucial: Niebuhrian pride, while frequently understood as a strictly arrogant and aggressive male problem, can also be problematic for nonaggressive men and for women. Pride means not so much that we are "full of ourselves" as that we are "preoccupied with ourselves." Stated differently, pride can be egotistic (inflated) or egoistic (self-obsessed). And it is crucial here to note that when Niebuhr uses the term "self-concern," he is in reality referring to *excessive* self-concern. Niebuhr believes that self-concern, like self-esteem, is very important. Our survival depends on self-regard. But in the face of anxiety, our temptation is to become excessively focused—even fixated—on ourselves. We develop an inordinate self-interest, a self-centeredness which unwittingly keeps us prisoners of our own efforts to affirm ourselves. As Niebuhr puts it, "Faith in the providence of God is a necessity of freedom because, without it, the anxiety of freedom tempts man to seek a self-sufficiency and self-mastery incompatible with his dependence upon forces which he does not control."[10]

Anxiety and Psychotherapy

For Niebuhr, as for Tillich, it is always the *total* self which is anxiously troubled. Estrangement reaches into every dimension of existence. Psychotherapy can of course help us with proximate goals and neurotic anxieties. Psychology can often heal what has been *psychologically* damaged. But psychology is not equipped to handle the ultimate dilemma of life because it *participates in that dilemma*. There is not a "part" of human existence which can redeem the other part. The story of human history has been one long tale of humanity trying to eradicate itself from its own destructiveness. Yet in spite of the utter failure of these multitude self-healing attempts, humanity nevertheless thinks it can fix things tomorrow. For Niebuhr, "no cumulation of contradictory evidence seems to disturb modern man's good opinion of himself."[11] Yet this optimism hides a deeper anxiety, "for under the perpetual smile of modernity there is a grimace of disillusion and cynicism."[12] And further:

> The final sin of man, said Luther truly, is his unwillingness to concede that he is a sinner. The significant contribution of modern culture to this perennial human inclination lies in the number of plausible reasons which it was able to adduce in support of man's good opinion of himself. The fact that many of these reasons stand in contradiction to each other did not shatter modern man's confidence in them; for he could always persuade himself of the truth of at least one of them and it never occurred to him that they might all be false.[13]

Make no mistake, both Niebuhr and Tillich would tell anyone struggling with neurotic anxiety such a phobias, social anxiety, panic

---

[10]Niebuhr, *Nature and Destiny of Man* 1:271.
[11]Niebuhr, *Nature and Destiny of Man* 1:94.
[12]Niebuhr, *Nature and Destiny of Man* 1:121.
[13]Niebuhr, *Nature and Destiny of Man* 1:121-22.

attacks, posttraumatic stress, or obsessive-compulsive behavior to visit the best psychotherapist they know. But like Kierkegaard, they are primarily interested in a form of anxiety which is "left over" even after we have cleared up our neurotic anxiety. Again, this is the anxiety of simply being human, of realizing that our choices define our future, and that we are all going to die. This is the anxiety of nonbeing pressing on being, the realization that our temporal existence has a deadline. This anxiety cannot be "therapized" or "drugged" away. It is connected with a sense of responsibility for our lives and our choices. Again, this existential anxiety is not itself the problem, but it certainly provokes either a self-reliance or a dependence on our Source. Niebuhr, as his famous "Serenity Prayer" suggests, believes we are indeed capable and responsible for changing many things in our lives. For these things he certainly believes in human effort and hard work. But there are other things which are clearly beyond our control. Because we are capable of self-consciousness and can thereby raise questions about the ultimate meaning and purpose of our lives, we will inevitably experience anxiety. And this form of anxiety is not something we can "conquer." It is this form of anxiety which can lead to our trust in God. However, it is also this form of anxiety which can lead us toward a frenzied attempt to find a form of self-security, to solve an infinite problem with finite resources. Niebuhr is quite frank on this point: This is a form of anxiety which can only be dealt with by a trust in the providence of God.

> An overweening or absolute trust in our own individual or communal power, in our intellect, in our righteousness, in our way of life, constitutes the pride that is unwarranted and destructive and is the essence of sin, as it is the deepest clue to the travail of history. Consequently only if the self can locate its trust in something genuinely transcendent to the self and to human achievement, individual or social, can it become itself. Faith as the deepest trust in and commitment to God is the condition of the possibility of love and so of justice and peace.[14]

At the risk of sounding repetitive, I want to reemphasize a central point: Niebuhr did not think self-regard is a bad thing. It is only *excessive* self-regard which pulls us into a world of greater and greater attempts to anchor our lives in a self-created security. It is not self-focus but *undue* self-focus with which Niebuhr has a problem. Put in more psychological terms,

---

[14]Gilkey, *On Niebuhr*, 25.

Niebuhr has absolutely no objection to the development of healthy self-esteem or a sense of self-confidence. But like Karen Horney, Niebuhr believed that this confidence will be based on a realistic assessment of ourselves and not on imaginary qualities we attribute to ourselves.[15] For Horney, we often create an idealized picture of who we "should be" and then go about a process of convincing ourselves that this is who we really are. Great energies are expended trying to maintain this highly inflated self-portrait. But this is part of what she calls "neurotic pride," rather than genuine self-confidence.[16] Similarly, Niebuhr holds a negative view toward exaggerated self-estimation which is not grounded in reality. Stated differently, *Niebuhr is opposed to excessive focus on the ego, not antagonistic to the process of having an ego.* His appreciation of individuality can be seen in his perennial battle with mysticism. For Niebuhr, mysticism, in seeking an undifferentiated ultimate reality, inevitably regards individuality or particularity as evil or a great obstacle to our ultimate connection with all that is. If we get rid of the ego, we can get rid of the problem. Mysticism encourages an elimination of the self through a merger with undifferentiated, ultimate reality. The self is left behind as it is absorbed into the divine. The singular is lost into the universal. But for Niebuhr, the ego is no illusion. Nor is it something we need to escape. Also, a problem with this "mystical union with all that is" is that we lose a sense of personal responsibility. There is nothing evil about being an individual. Niebuhr carried a lifelong disdain for pantheism. As he puts it:

> Mysticism always regards the final depth of human consciousness as in some sense identical with the eternal order, and believes that men may know God if they penetrate deeply enough into the mystery of their own being. But on the other hand the transcendent God of biblical faith makes himself known in the finite and historical world. The finite world is not, because of its finiteness, incapable of entertaining comprehensible revelations of the incomprehensible God.[17]

This is important to emphasize because Niebuhr never advocated the denial of human needs in an attempt to become totally other-centered. A

---

[15]Karen Horney, *Neurosis and Human Growth* (New York: W. W. Norton, 1950) chap. 1.

[16]Horney, *Neurosis and Human Growth*, chap. 4.

[17]Niebuhr, *Nature and Destiny of Man* 1:126.

responsible desire to meet our own needs is not the same as a frantic self-concern which disregards the needs of others. There is no virtue in self-neglect. The refusal to be a self is as problematic as an excessive focus on the self. Individuality is fine; a belief in radical self-sufficiency is not.

Thus, for Niebuhr, we *really are* insecure. Our insecurity is not a psychological distortion. It is our essential nature. We are ontologically or structurally anxious. This is our fundamental makeup. It is a mistake to turn *this* level of insecurity into a psychological problem which can be therapized and healed. It cannot be psychologically cured.

Yet, once again, this anxiety or insecurity which is an essential part of our being does not *have* to be a problem. It becomes a problem because we distrust God and attempt to resolve it ourselves. Pride denies the contingencies of life, turns the self into a god, and thereby creates unjust relations with others. It is always a defense and a cover-up for ontological anxiety. Niebuhr is consistently clear that in between our essential anxiety and pride is this element of *distrust*. This distrust in God is always involved in the elevation of ourselves. In that sense, distrust *precedes* pride. Everyone is anxious, whether they admit it or not. They may experience little conscious anxiety because they believe they are immune from finitude is therefore strong. Put simply, we are extremely clever in denying what scares the hell out of us. Yet no amount of pretension will eradicate this deeper sense of vulnerability. And again, this not simply the vulnerability of low self-esteem or inadequate self-regard. It is not an anxiety *caused* by deficient psychological processes. This insecurity is not a cognitive error, not an unresolved childhood issue, and not something we can eliminate in psychotherapy. *It is the human condition pure and simple.*

So if one asks Niebuhr: Isn't your pride a defense, a cover-up for a deeper form of insecurity, he would say, "Of course." But this deeper form of insecurity is not a purely psychological malady which can be cured through treatment. It is instead the essential and structural anxiety of the human condition. It is not psychologically constructed; it is ontologically given. Thus, for Niebuhr, because our insecurity and anxiety are not self-caused, they cannot be self-corrected. We're not anxious because of some unfortunate misreading of our experience. We are anxious, at least in an ontological sense, because we have *correctly* interpreted that experience. Again, when we assume that anxiety has a purely psychological explanation, the next step is to say that it has a psychological cure.

With the right techniques, we can eliminate our fundamental insecurity.

But existential anxiety is not the child of pathology. We don't create our own insecurity. It is not psychologically manufactured. Nor is it merely the result of an external cause which can be changed. In a sense, some psychologists both *underestimate* the problem of insecurity, and *overestimate* our ability to resolve it. Carl Rogers tell us that we wouldn't feel anxious if we weren't incongruent; Heinz Kohut tells us that we wouldn't feel anxious if our parents had not empathically failed us; Albert Ellis tells us that we wouldn't feel anxious if we thought more rationally. But these approaches do not recognize that *our very situation as human beings produces anxiety*. The only way to stop being anxious is to stop being human.

The Human Paradox

For Niebuhr, the human condition is both anxious and paradoxical. Often sounding much like Pascal, Niebuhr believes that if we don't see this tension between two opposing elements in humanity, we will surely develop a one-sided picture. In fact, Gilkey, in his study of Niebuhr, very helpfully identifies four major paradoxes which Niebuhr regularly emphasizes.[18] The first of these paradoxes is that human beings are *both* a part of nature (sharing a connection with other animals), and they are also self-transcendent and made in the "image" of God. Viewing the Genesis account as a symbolic story about our current relationship with God rather than as a depiction of a historical or scientific beginning, Niebuhr had no problems accepting Darwin's conclusions about our evolutionary past. Yet accompanying this natural evolution is a human capacity to step outside of ourselves and reflect on the meaning of our existence. We are finite beings with the capacity to long for infinity; temporal beings with a taste for eternity. These two elements, as we have already noted, are completely intertwined. If we try to separate them and develop an ill-advised dualism, we will no longer grasp the essence of being human. Whether it is a mind/body dualism, a spirit/flesh dualism, or a material/spiritual dualism, we will miss the point. What is crucial to grasp, especially for the purposes of a dialogue with psychology, is that *finitude itself is never the problem*. Following Friedrich Scheiermacher and many other post-Enlightenment theologians, Niebuhr did not believe that physical death is a punishment for the sin of the first couple. Natural death was part of the picture when

---

[18]Gilkey, *On Niebuhr*, 80-81.

humanity arrived on the scene. Nothing connected to finitude—our bodies, our limited minds, our mortality, or our temporality—are the sources of sin. Over and over again, Niebuhr reminds us that if sin is inherently built into finitude, then none of us can be held responsible for what we do. Sin would be necessitated in the same way that breathing is required. Our conditioned lives, however much we might like to escape them, do not *cause* us to act in destructive ways. Even in this limited, anxious world there is nothing preventing us from trusting God.

Along with this "creaturely status" which involves a full immersion in biological existence, human beings are also self-transcendent. Traditionally, Greek thought located the notion of an "image of God" in our capacities for reason. The mind represents the image of God. Conversely, in later rather than classical Greek thought, the body represents the great obstacle to the development of the mind. The body is material, this-worldly, and corrupt. In fact, the mind is "trapped" in the body, a most unfortunate imprisonment from which it seeks escape. Niebuhr completely rejected this notion that reason is heavenly while the rest of the body is evil. He believed very strongly that this Manichaean emphasis on material corruption contradicted the Judeo-Christian conviction that creation is "good."

In what may well be the best paragraph of his entire book on Niebuhr, Gilkey puts this issue very insightfully. Though lengthy, it is worth quoting.

> There is no aspect of our creaturely, organic life that is not transmuted by spirit. Freedom transforms the given of natural instincts, for example, sexuality, into a wide variety of diverse cultural forms, into the highest levels of human relatedness and mutuality (eros and philios), into the capacity, uniquely human, of destructive perversity, and finally into the transcendent possibility of a love that is self-forgetful (agape). Correspondingly, the natural or organic communal relatedness of family, clan, and community are given by spirit the possibility of their infinitely various cultural forms in history, the continually destructive possibilities of social idolatry and oppression, whether in family or community, and the final possibilities of justice transmuted by love: the kingdom of God. The natural orders of animal existence are thus continually broken and refashioned by spirit into an infinity of customs and mores both at the instant when human beings (hominids) first appeared and throughout their subsequent historical development. History is the transformation of nature of nature—of creatureliness—by freedom, and yet

history never ceases to remain nature at its base.[19]

Stated simply, nature and spirit cannot and will not leave each other alone. Their destiny is a unified one.

A second paradox of the human condition is that we are on the one hand responsible, moral, and seek to do the good, but on the other hand, we are universally destructive, sometimes cruel, and self-centered. This fundamental ambiguity in the human condition must be acknowledged if we are to have a realistic view of history and human nature. We need not be as cynical as Hobbes, but we also need not be as optimistic as Rousseau. The pendulum swings back and forth from era to era. Certainly within psychology, we can see this shift occurring in a dramatic manner. Freud riveted the highly optimistic and progressive view of civilized human beings with a rather dark portrait of hostile wishes and sexual forces. Later, humanistic psychologists such as Carl Rogers and Abraham Maslow invited a radical move away from a focus on psychopathology and argued that human beings are basically good and positively directed. And in many posthumanistic circles, humanistic psychologists are often portrayed as too individualistic, too naïve and gullible about human goodness, and therefore lopsided in their thinking about the human condition. Yet others are now turning again to a more optimistic view as a part of what is frequently termed "positive psychology." In the midst of these opposing perspectives, perhaps it is time to say once again with both Niebuhr and Tillich that human beings are thoroughly ambiguous. They are not fated by nature to act in destructive ways, yet they inevitably seem to distort their freedom and act unjustly toward each other.

Another paradox Gilkey mentions, which is sprinkled throughout Niebuhr's writings, is that while human beings have a deep thirst for meaning and purpose, they also often despair. The struggle for significance is universal and yet so is the frequent feelings of insignificance. We long to live forever but feel the cold reality of death marching behind us. We want to establish something of lasting significance and yet our brief lives sometimes pass in front of us. Blaise Pascal, whose grasp of the human paradox greatly influenced Niebuhr, put this issue famously:

> This is our true state; this is what makes us capable of certain knowledge and of absolute ignorance. We sail within a vast sphere, ever drifting in uncertainty,

[19]Gilkey, *On Niebuhr*, 88.

driven from end to end. When we think to attach ourselves to any point and to fasten to it, it wavers and leaves us; and if we follow it, it eludes our grasp, slips past us, and vanishes forever. Nothing stays for us. This is our natural condition, and yet most contrary to our inclination; we burn with desire to find solid ground and an ultimate sure foundation whereon to build a tower reaching to the Infinite. But our whole groundwork cracks, and the earth opens to abysses.[20]

These paradoxes of human experience can be found in psychology, literature, philosophy, art, sociology, and almost any conception of human personhood. This greatness and wretchedness seem to coexist regardless of how much we'd like to disprove one or the other.

And finally, human beings seem on the one hand determined, and yet on the other hand responsible for our own actions. Our deepest sense of ourselves seems to involve being both determined and yet free. This is not a paradox found only in theological conceptions. It is true of almost any perspective in the social sciences. Few are willing to go so far as B.F. Skinner and proclaim that freedom is an utter illusion and that none of us are responsible for our own actions. For Skinner, the environment is all determining.[21] But for most social scientists, and for most judicial systems, the assumption of human responsibility is a constant. Even if external or unconscious factors have strong influence on our behavior, we are nevertheless responsible, unless of course we are deemed incapable of determining the difference between right or wrong. But the insanity defense is notoriously unsuccessful. We each carry a sense of guilt or an "uneasy conscience."

As I have already mentioned, it's important to emphasize this primary paradox in Niebuhr's view of humanity because he has sometimes been categorized as either too negative or too positive in his evaluation of the human condition. Humanists and theological liberals no doubt find his analysis far too pessimistic. They would argue that Niebuhr finds excessive self-regard behind every bush and does not recognize the potential for which humanity is capable. Theological conservatives, on the other hand, particularly those who still read the fall of Adam and Eve literally and historically—which includes a lot of people in our world—would find Niebuhr too optimistic in so far as he refuses to believe we carry the inherited "taint"

---

[20]Blaise Pascal, *Pensees* (New York: Random House, 1941) 25.
[21]B. F. Skinner, *Beyond Freedom and Dignity* (New York: Bantam, 1971).

of original sin from Adam. I can remember doing a presentation on Niebuhr to a group of very conservative Calvinists whom I thought would appreciate Niebuhr's scathing analysis of the deceptiveness of human sin. But instead, they immediately focused on Niebuhr's nonliteralistic account of the Fall and pointed out that he was far too optimistic about the human condition. In fact, Niebuhr was called a "Pelagian" in so far as he interpreted the Adamic story symbolically and held out that human beings do not come into this world with a preexisting corruption. I would have never guessed that Niebuhr would have been tagged an optimist!

Yet as Gilkey points out, there *is* a sense in which Niebuhr follows the fifth-century monk, Pelagius. Pelagius argued passionately against Augustine that Adam's sin affected only Adam. It did not biologically "taint" anyone else in the sense that the rest of humanity came into the world with a bad blueprint. Of course Adam set a horrible example. Of course he introduced sin into the world. But he did not *cause* any of his descendents to sin. We are not "born into" sin in the way Augustine thought. We inherit a world full of sin, but our nature is not fundamentally distorted before we take our first breath. Niebuhr would agree that Adam's sin tells our story but is not the direct cause of our sin. While Niebuhr obviously deliteralized and dehistorcized Adam while Pelagius surely believed in the historical concreteness of the first couple, Niebuhr would agree with Pelagius that our essential nature is not corrupted by Adam's deed. Beyond this, however, Niebuhr and Pelagius are in profound *disagreement* on many issues.

For purposes of intellectual honesty, it is important to realize that the vast majority of people from all walks of life and academic disciplines took the Adam and Eve story *literally* before the Enlightenment. This historical doctrine of original sin was taken in a nonsymbolic way. It did indeed describe the situation of the first couple and largely went unquestioned as the historical *cause* of evil. This was certainly true of moral evil, and many also believed it explained natural evil. In other words, prior to Adam's dastardly deed, there was no violence and death in the natural world either. Adam's misdeed brought death into the world.

With the rise of our knowledge about the long history of the universe and our planet, along with our understanding of the slow evolutionary process, it no longer became possible to explain the world based on a literal account of this story. It must be read symbolically and allegorically. While most theologians working with the Genesis materials long ago accepted this symbolic interpretation, it is a fact—even if an embarrassing one—that many religious people *still* read the Creation story as a factual, literal, and historical account. Perhaps it is important to state categorically that Niebuhr would not dignify such a belief as a "paradox" or "mystery." Instead he would flatly call it an absurdity and a contradiction of everything we know about science. Put another way, I don't think Niebuhr would have much patience with Creation Science. Niebuhr would surely say that a very insightful story which conveys a powerful insight about human nature is being reduced to biological and historical nonsense. For Niebuhr, one of the greatest obstacles to the deep truth of the Adamic story is the ridiculous notion that it is a factual account of sin's beginnings. Fundamentalists will find no more of an ally in Niebuhr than they find in Tillich. And further, the Church's literalization of the Genesis account involves placing Adam in a completely different situation than we are in. For according to this tradition, only Adam was truly "free." The rest of us, because of Adam's vile deed are born into a situation of "nonfreedom" in which sin is a necessary part of our being. "For Niebuhr we are each as close to original sin as were Adam and Eve; they are symbols of what we do."[22]

For Niebuhr, then, sin is a distortion of our essential structure, not the loss of that structure. In other words, nothing within the human package fates us to sin. If that were so, we would obviously not be responsible. Stated another way, there is nothing *inherently* wrong with us. The "Fall" does not refer to a past historical "event" but to an ever-present reality. The "Fall" does not explain the origin of sin; it instead describes our own experience in the here and now. Again, the literalization of this symbolic story leads to an absurdity.

Contrary to Freud, Niebuhr did not believe that our destructive inclinations are rooted in our biology. There is no natural inclination toward excessive aggression or sexual preoccupation. When these drives are out of control, it signifies a distortion of our basic nature rather than an expression of it. In fact, as we will later see in our exploration of Niebuhr and psychoanalysis, Niebuhr, like Tillich, had a very interesting and nuanced perspective on psychoanalysis. On the one hand, he applauded Freud's realism about the human condition. One might even say that Freud was a masterful interpreter of our estranged condition. But Freud did not tell us about our *essential* condition. In other words, to borrow Tillich's term,

---

[22]Gilkey, *On Niebuhr*, 137.

Freud described estranged existence, an existence which refused to conform to the essential structure of being human. Freud spoke powerfully about our actual existence, but he made the mistake of assuming that our predicament is rooted in our biological life. For Freud, the conflicts we experience in life are a permanent and necessary fixture of our existence. It could not have been otherwise. In fact, his final picture of the life instinct (*eros*) vs. the death instinct (*thanatos*) is a psychological rendition of the dualism found in Zoroastrianism. It is a permanent, ineradicable dualism, a battle for which there is no final healing. While Niebuhr applauds the vivid insights of our destructive tendencies, he believes that Freud attributes those tendencies to the wrong source, namely our biology. In fact, it is here that Freud and fundamentalist perspectives on inherited sin make strange bedfellows. For both perspectives, "sin" simply must happen. It is now, at least since Adam, built into human finitude. Adam no longer "tells" our story; he "caused" our story.

Niebuhr thus agrees with many neo-Freudian positions which refuse to locate human destructiveness within our biology. Clearly the majority of post-Freudians have given up a belief in the death instinct. Yet Niebuhr disagrees with the optimism inherent in many post-Freudians because he sees a return to an excessive optimism. Put more directly, Niebuhr disagrees with the frequent neo-Freudian position that humanity can clean up its own estrangement problem on its own. Erich Fromm, as we shall later see, is a classic example of someone who wrote powerfully about human destructiveness yet held out the possibility that humanity could eventually bring about a utopian world of full consciousness.[23] Destructiveness can ultimately be overcome by greater self-awareness. For Niebuhr, this form of self-rescue, apart from a dependence on our Source, is impossible. As Tillich might put it, there is no "unestranged" part of us which can heal the rest of our estranged condition.[24] "Total depravity" does *not* mean that we

---

[23]See Erich Fromm, *The Heart of Man: Its Genius for Good and Evil* (New York: Harper & Row, 1964); *The Anatomy of Human Destructiveness* (New York: Henry Holt, 1973). For an excellent theological critique of Fromm's perspective on overcoming estrangement, see Guy Hammond, *Man in Estrangement: A Comparison of the Thought of Paul Tillich and Erich Fromm* (Nashville: Vanderbilt University Press, 1965).

[24]For a fuller account of Tillich's perspective on this point, see my *Paul Tillich and Psychology* (Macon GA: Mercer University Press, 2006).

are as bad as we can possibly be, but it *does mean* that there is no part of our lives which remains unaffected by our estrangement and excessive self-regard. Our created structure, which Niebuhr calls our "original righteousness" is distorted. As Gilkey puts it,

> because of sin (the inescapable self-concern that insinuates itself into all our natural relations), each of these—sensual love, mutual love, and even communal justice—is prone to become less than loving and less than just. Sensual love is corrupted by inordinate self-love, and the other is uses as an object; mutual love quickly descends into calculation about how really "mutual" it is, a calculation dominated by a self-interest worried it is being used by the other; any concrete scheme of justice expresses an uneasy and unequal balance of power among persons and among groups in a community, a balance in which one side can easily dominate and in so doing defeat the desire to achieve real justice.[25]

Obviously sin is already in the world before any of us make our own choices. And obviously that sin greatly influences each of us. But we cannot be completely exonerated because of our "sinful surroundings." Perhaps this is another paradox within Niebuhr, and one that makes him an interesting source of dialogue with psychology. He accents individual responsibility while understanding the powerful tug of social and historical location. His contextualization of our behavior does not eliminate our responsibility for that behavior. We are both victims and participants. Yet our victimization is not so strong that it eliminates altogether our own culpability. This helps Niebuhr resist the Marxist dichotomy between the oppressed and the oppressors. Certainly the oppressed perpetuate more destructiveness and are therefore more responsible. This is what Nieubuhr meant by his rather famous phrase, "the equality of sin but the inequality of guilt." While no one, according to Niebuhr, rises completely above the world of excessive self-regard, some are clearly more "guilty" than others in so far as they bring about far greater suffering and oppression to others. Put differently, some people are far more destructive than others. Yet Niebuhr refuses to therefore say that the oppressed are completely innocent and, if put in positions of power, would never act in destructive ways. The extent of our destructiveness is often an outgrowth of the extent of our power. Thus Niebuhr rises against all forms of "us" and "them" thinking,

---

[25]Gilkey, *On Niebuhr*, 99.

especially when it presents our own aims as 100% pure and the aims of the other as one-hundred-percent evil.

> How quickly the poor, the weak, the deprived of yesterday, may, on gaining a social victory over their detractors, exhibit the same arrogance and the same will to power that which they abhorred in their opponents and which they were inclined to regard as a congenital sin of their enemies. . . . This is the self-righteousness of the weak as opposed to the self-righteousness of the powerful.[26]

The minute we believe that our group represents a pure form of humanity, a more righteous crowd which can completely resolve the human dilemma once we are in charge, we are engaging in a self-righteous delusion.

At times, Niebuhr's perspective may appear to be utterly contradictory. On the one hand, we are not fated to act in destructive ways. On the other hand, we inevitably do. There is nothing built into the structure of our being which "makes us" act in unloving, self-centered, and unjust ways. Yet everyone does it. Is this not an absurd contradiction, an impossible description? It would certainly seem that way. Yet Niebuhr would quickly add: Does it not describe our own experience? Does it not point toward the paradoxical relationship between freedom and destiny? And Niebuhr might quickly add that this paradox will also emerge in any realistic secular analysis of the human dilemma. It is therefore not some illogical theological position imposed on the human condition; instead, it is an apt description of the deepest experience of ourselves in the world.

Niebuhr believed that the work of Freud and psychoanalysis greatly enriched an understanding of the human condition, and particularly the human capacity for self-deception. Throughout his life, Niebuhr appreciated and engaged psychoanalytic thought. Let us therefore examine Niebuhr and depth psychology.

---

[26]Niebuhr, *Nature and Destiny of Man* 1:226.

3

Niebuhr and Depth Psychology

[T]he conscious or rational ego is never the simple master of the self.
—Reinhold Niebuhr

Niebuhr affirmed and appreciated what is often called "depth psychology," the exploration of the underlying, unconscious conflicts which often shape our conscious reason. In fact, Niebuhr believed that depth psychology offered a new vocabulary for describing excessive self-regard. In this chapter, I will bring Niebuhr into discussion with four prominent depth psychologists: Sigmund Freud, Carl Jung, Karen Horney, and Erich Fromm.

Niebuhr and Freud

Reinhold Niebuhr and Sigmund Freud share a profound ability to take the mask off things and look at the unpleasantries beneath that mask. To say that neither took things at face value is an understatement. Niebuhr greatly appreciates Freud, and like his colleague Tillich, believes that Freud has provided some extremely important insights into the human condition. Freud, for Niebuhr, is a great scientific innovator and clinical genius. In an essay devoted to Freud's insights, Niebuhr says, "By laying bare the intricate mechanism of the self's inner debate with itself, and its labrynthian depths below the level of consciousness, he enlarged or indeed created new methods of healing 'mental' diseases."[1] In spite of his acknowledgement of these clinical insights, however, Niebuhr is much more interested in Freud as a theorist of human nature. Niebuhr wants to bring to the forefront the implicit image of the person in Freudian psychoanalysis. He therefore investigated Freud's picture of the human dilemma, its possibilities, and how we might go about achieving that end.

Niebuhr reminds us that prior to Freud, the Enlightenment had all but

---

[1]Reinhold Niebuhr, "Human Creativity and Self-Concern in Freud's Thought," in *Freud and the 20th Century*, ed. Benjamin Nelson (New York: Meridian Books, 1957) 259.

ruled out any emphasis on a hidden "corruption" in humanity. There was no accent on the significance of excessive self-regard as problematic. As he puts it:

> From Renaissance to Enlightenment, which was indeed the climax of the Renaissance, the one unifying factor in otherwise diverse philosophies, whether naturalistic or idealistic was the favorable view of the potentialities of human nature and the confidence that any residual capacity for evil in man could be eliminated progressively if either nature or reason could be man's guide.[2]

Whether this evil was to be eliminated by the conquering resources of reason or the Romantic return to nature, the point is that evil *could* be, and eventually *would* be, overcome. As I have previously mentioned, this Enlightenment perspective was dominated by a double optimism: (a) human beings are basically good, and (b) human history is progressing morally. The last vestiges of our primitive inclinations will eventually be completely overcome. While human nature has experienced a "cultural lag," this condition will soon be corrected. Reason can be trusted as an objective means of redemption. Our moral compass is completely intact. We need only to further this belief in ourselves and allow this wonderful progress to unfold.

Freud profoundly interrupted humanity's smooth confidence in itself. Again and again, Freud argued that our civilized reason is often driven by underlying, not-so-pretty factors of which we are not even aware. While we have a strong, invested interest in seeing ourselves in a positive light, something dark is nevertheless going on backstage. Our motives do not match our pure pretensions. We are far more aggressive, selfish, and sexual than we realize. Thus, most of our thinking is a conscious masquerade to hide what is happening unconsciously. The outrage triggered by Freud's naked revealing of the prim and proper Victorian personality makes it easy to see why he acquired the title, "master of suspicion." We are hardly as reasonable or as moral as we'd like to think.

For Niebuhr, Freud offered a new vocabulary for discussing a very outdated notion—original sin. Granted this was a secularized view of original sin; nevertheless, Freud's realistic view of internal human conflict offered new conceptual tools with which to discuss this old doctrine. In a sense,

---

[2]Niebuhr, "Human Creativity and Self Concern in Freud," 260.

Freud was both a child of the Enlightenment and its greatest critic. He argued that the Enlightenment conception of the governing control of reason is most naïve. What seemed to be sophisticated cerebral habits of a cultured person were in fact pushed, pulled, and driven by rather impolite impulses. Niebuhr believes that Freud gave us the "first realist account of human behavior."[3] Freud's tripartite theory of the self and its conflicts (id, ego, and superego) enormously challenged the old, simpler dualistic view which pitted mind against body. This older dualism had become optimistic because of its hope that mind would eventually control everything. Niebuhr describes this dualism.

> This dualism was informed by the assumption that the mind, if powerful enough or educated sufficiently, would be in control of all its impulses and it would guide the self to the more inclusive rational ends which constituted the uniquely human aspects of man's life, as distinguished from animals, who lived merely in the dimensions of nature.[4]

Enlightenment science, therefore, can usher in a world free of injustice. Thus, reason can have a "pure" quality. It can be a salvific instrument which can transcend its own interests and offer an unbiased means of bringing about a harmonious world. Yet this perspective does not take seriously the possibility that reason itself can be the tool of personal or class interests. The Enlightenment mentality thinks it can empty itself of preconceptions and presuppositions and allow critical reason to perform its unblemished and objective tasks.

For Freud, however, reason is often completely unaware of the grip that human instincts hold on it. Put simply, the human mind can convince itself or nearly anything. We regularly hide the truth about ourselves, ignore sexual and aggressive elements in our behavior, and frequently live only on the surface of life. The human mind has further convinced itself that evolutionary progress also means *moral* progress. Rather than saying that human life is simply evolving toward greater complexity, many want to see it as evolving toward a higher morality. Yet as Niebuhr puts it, "the conscious or rational ego is never the simple master of the self."[5] This Freudian view of rationality therefore undermines Kant's notion that a

---

[3] Niebuhr, "Human Creativity and Self-Concern in Freud," 260.
[4] Niebuhr, "Human Creativity and Self-Concern in Freud," 261.
[5] Niebuhr, "Human Creativity and Self-Concern in Freud," 263.

godlike reason can impose and demand duty from our natural inclinations. And Freud especially challenged Hegel's notion that human reason can extract itself from its particularities and become "one" with a disembodied, universal rationality.

While there is no evidence that Freud read Thomas Hobbes, an interesting comparison can be made between them. Hobbes, prior to Freud, rejected any optimism about the human condition.[6] In fact, Hobbes argued that human reason can never emancipate itself from the undercurrents of selfish ambition. As Niebuhr puts it, "Men's reason is not for Hobbes the instrument for lifting them above themselves and viewing their interests from some universally valid perspective. It is the servant of the self's interests and passions."[7]

Yet Niebuhr believes that neither Enlightenment optimism nor Hobbesian pessimism adequately describe reason's ambiguities. Reason contains both creative and destructive possibilities. We can use our reason to put our own wishes in a larger perspective or we can use our reason as the servant for selfish ambitions. We can further spin out elaborate justifications to hide the selfish aims behind our behavior. While believing Hobbes's conclusions were too cynical, Niebuhr nevertheless thinks Hobbes saw something very important, namely, that "reason is never completely emancipated from the particular and parochial interests of the individual and collective particular."[8] Hobbes's extremely pessimistic view necessitates a political absolutism which will suppress the ever-present possibility of anarchy. Democracy, argues Niebuhr, would not have been possible if Locke and others had not shown that reason can be used for the sake of justice as well as injustice.

The Life Instinct and the Death Instinct

In *Civilization and It's Disconcontents*, Freud clearly states his conviction that there are ultimately two ultimate instincts, *eros* and *thanatos*, which are at war with each other. He says:

> I adopt the standpoint, therefore, that the inclination to aggression is an

---

[6]Thomas Hobbes, *Leviathan* (1651), Norton Critical Edition, ed. Richard E. Flathman and David Johnston (New York: W. W. Norton, 1996).

[7]Niebuhr, "Human Creativity and Self-Concern in Freud," 267.

[8]Niebuhr, "Human Creativity and Self-Concern in Freud," 268.

original, self-subsisting instinctual disposition in man, and I return to my view that it constitutes the greatest impediment to civilization. . . . I may now add that civilization is a process in the service of Eros, whose purpose is to combine single human individuals, and after that families, then races, peoples and nations, into one great unity, the unity of mankind. Why this has to happen we do not know; the work of Eros is precisely this. These collections of men are to be libidinally bound to one another. Necessity alone, the advantages of work in common, will not hold them together. But man's natural aggressive instinct, the hostility toward of each against all and of all against each, opposes the programme of civilization. This aggressive instinct is the derivative of and the main representative of the death instinct which we have found alongside of Eros and which shares world dominion with it. And now, I think, the meaning of the evolution of civilization is no longer obscure to us. It must present the struggle between Eros and Death, between the instinct of life and the instinct destruction, as it works itself out in the human species. This struggle is what all life essentially consists of, and the evolution of civilization may therefore be simply described as the struggle for life and the human species. And it is this battle of the giants that our nursemaids try to appease with their lullaby about Heaven.[9]

For Freud, two cosmic forces are doing battle and there is no hint of an end in sight. In fact, Freud's final perspective on this eros vs. thanatos battle flatly contradicts any nineteenth-century notion of progress. His belief in science and his hope for better understanding the unconscious dimensions of life are met with a formidable, unconquerable foe—the death instinct. Freud admits that he was quite reluctant to come to this conclusion. And further, he is not surprised that others find this idea most distasteful. "For little children do not like it when there is talk of the inborn inclination toward 'badness,' to aggressiveness and destructiveness, and so to cruelty as well."[10]

Niebuhr objects to Freud's division of life into *eros* and *thanatos*, a division Niebuhr thinks is similar to the older Greek dualism of mind and body. In response to Freud's postulation of two drives constantly at war with each other, Niebuhr makes the following rather interesting remark:

The idea that a separate and distinct death impulse operates mysteriously in

---

[9]Sigmund Freud, *Civilization and Its Discontents*, trans. James Srachey (W. W. Norton, 1961) 69.

[10]Freud, *Civilization and Its Discontents*, 67.

conflict with the life impulse has the virtue of calling attention to the dynamic character of evil in the world. But every social situation proves that an impulse of sheer destruction exists only among psychopaths. In normal life the death impulse is in the service of the life impulse or flows from it inadvertently. Neither animal nor men kill out of sheer love of destruction. They kill to maintain their own life. They destroy the foe only when he challenges the community which Eros has established. Evil, in other words, is much more inextricably bound with up with good than is comprehended in this psychology or in any of the modern substitutes for analysis of prophetic Christianity.[11]

Typically, Niebuhr resists any dichotomy which makes good and evil look as if they can be easily divided. Instead, life is much too ambiguous for such easy divisions. Again, following Luther, he would say that we are always saint and sinner.

We need, however, to be very careful with Niebuhr's interpretation of this Freudian "dualism." Freud insisted that the life instinct and death instinct have separate sources of energy, *but he did not believe that they appear in "pure" forms.* They are instead always mixed. As Freud put it, "the two kinds of instinct seldom—perhaps never—appear in isolation from each other, but are alloyed with each other in varying and different proportions and so become unrecognizable to our judgment."[12] In other words, the two drives appear intermingled and not as pure states. Indeed, it would have been a shocking surprise if Freud had thought otherwise. After all, he had been the great pioneer of pulling the curtain on human goodness and showing that it is never far from destructive elements. It was Freud, more than anyone, who had shown us that our best intentions are often accompanied by self-seeking motives. Thus, while Freud attributed two sources to the life instinct and death instinct, they are comingled in everyday existence.

Yet this intermingling of life and death instincts in human existence does not fully eliminate Niebuhr's concern. For ultimately, Freud *does* attribute everything which happens in the cosmos to two fundamentally different forces. As Browning and I have argued, this dualism reaches a cosmic proportion.[13] These forces do not simply divide the human mind;

---

[11]Reinhold Niebuhr, *An Interpretation of Christian Ethics* (New York: Harper & Row, 1935).

[12]Freud, *Civilization and Its Discontents*, 66.

[13]Browning and Cooper, *Religious Thought and the Modern Psychologies*,

instead, they are built into and influence *all* life. They become the metaphysical principle by which Freud interprets ultimate reality. Because Freud pushes these instincts into cosmic principles, he reveals a quasi-religious outlook. Eros and Thanatos become far more than a psychological hypothesis which helps interpret clinical data. They are ultimate explanatory principles for interpreting all of existence. They are metaphysical handles for Freud's world view. Life has been and always shall be in conflict. What at first may have been understood merely as an intrapsychic conflict turns out instead to be cosmic battle. This is the Freudian faith in the ultimate context of our lives. And as we shall see, it is one of the reasons Jung felt deeply unsatisfied with Freud's ultimate division of the cosmos, a split which is never finally healed.

Also, Freud's death instinct had both an active and passive dimension.[14] The active form of thanatos involved an aggression toward others or oneself. Externalized aggression obviously attacks others. War is a simple example. Yet if civilization is to be possible, some of humanity's natural aggressiveness must be blocked and turned back on itself. This can take the form of a harsh superego. As Freud put it, "civilization, therefore, obtains mastery over the individual's dangerous desire for aggression by weakening and disarming it and by setting up an agency within him to watch it, like a garrison in a conquered city."[15] The superego's aggressiveness against the ego thus keeps the aggression from moving outward onto others. This can lead toward a chronic sense of guilt and depression.

In the passive form, however, the aggression is not so easily identified. Organic life simply wants to return to inorganic life. In other words, the passive side of the death instinct seeks the ultimate tensionless state—death. This is the tug of inertia, the pull toward a kind of lifeless existence. This passive form of *thanatos* simply does not want to be "bothered" by life. It leads toward a quiet resignation, a retreat from the world of effort. In fact, it is quite similar to Niebuhr's understanding of sloth. It backs away from the burdens and responsibilities of full personhood. In order to kill the anxieties of life, it is willing to become lifeless. It is close to what Niebuhr

---

chap. 3.

[14]For a fuller theological discussion of Freud and human destructiveness, see my *Dimensions of Evil: Contemporary Perspectives* (Minneapolis: Fortress, 2007) esp. chap. 3.

[15]Freud, *Civilization and Its Discontents*, 70-71.

describes as the sin of self-escape or self-avoidance, the sin which liberation thinkers sometimes accuse Niebuhr of omitting.

But for Niebuhr, neither form of the death instinct is "built" within us as a natural, and therefore necessary, expression of our being. Evil and destructive behavior are not rooted in biology. They do not automatically occur due to the way we are hardwired. Instead, we *become* destructive of ourselves and others as we mishandle anxiety, fail to trust God, and make ourselves the center of life. We are not doomed to be excessively aggressive. *Thanatos* is not part of our inherent or created condition; instead, it is a distortion of that condition. We are not ontologically broken. Instead, our destructiveness grows out of anxiously excessive self-preoccupations. We cannot blame our biology for it. If we could, then human sin would be an illusion.

The Primary Freudian Mistake: "Biologizing" Destructiveness

Niebuhr held a very similar attitude toward both Augustine and Freud. Indeed, as we have seen, Freud in many ways offers a secular version of Augustinian original sin. Both Augustine and Freud captured what Niebuhr understood to be the tragic element of existence, a condition that good intensions or even an iron willpower could not cure. Just as Augustine had put his finger on the universal destiny of sin, so Freud had described the dark character of the unconscious. Yet, as we saw previously, Niebuhr clearly deliteralizes the Augustinian myth of sin's beginning and distances himself from any notion that sin is sexually transmitted. Similarly, while he applauds Freud's description of our destructive potential and the death instinct, he is quick to insist that this problem is not rooted in biology. For Freud, there is no rescue from the biologically rooted conflict between the life and death instinct. Put theologically, sin is both inevitable *and* necessary. The very structure of human life is such that destructive behavior will follow. Of course we can attempt to minimize it and make the most of it, but there is no ultimate healing of estrangement. Thus, Freud failed to separate humanity's existential and essential natures. Physical existence is a dark, destructive existence.

Yet Niebuhr would agree with Tillich's frequent comment that Freud's concept of estranged existence is a "gift" to Christian theology. It helps move theologians away from static and moralistic conceptions of sin. In fact, some of the neo-Freudians have moved away from the master's

Augustinian pessimism and have become much more Pelagian in their optimism about humanity resolving its estrangement problem. These approaches suggest that we can, on the basis of our own efforts, heal our ultimate predicament. Healthier forms of parenting, the right sort of environment, greater educational opportunities, more equal distributions of wealth, or even universal psychotherapy can "end" our estrangement difficulty. We can "manage" the human condition through our own efforts. While psychotherapy can help us clear the runway of many neurotic elements, Niebuhr believes it is not equipped to address and heal the larger questions of meaning, purpose, and value.

Niebuhr's persrpective on the neo-Freudian position concerning human destructiveness is also very similar to Tillich's. If Freud's *etiology* of human destructiveness is mistaken, then so too, is the common neo-Freudian *prognosis* of the human condition. While Niebuhr believed that Freud is mistaken when he assumes that human destructiveness emerges from our biology, he is also critical of the frequent neo-Freudian assertion that this tendency toward destructiveness is psychologically caused, and can therefore be psychologically eradicated. Niebuhr's comment on the neo-Freudians is most interesting:

> The Neo-Freudians have sought to correct what was regarded as a too purely "biological" approach to Freud. The have emphasized the lack of love and security in the home as the cause of neuroses (Harry Stack: *Interpersonal Psychiatry*). Or they have found the cause of mental illness in the cultural situation, as for instance in the insecurities of a capitalist order (Karen Horney: *The Neurotic Personality of Our Time* and *Neurosis and Human Growth*). Or they have taken Freud's dim attitude toward the superego so seriously that they have derived human ills from the moral demands made upon the self and thus reduced Freudianism to another version of the physiocratic thesis that human egoism would be harmless if not repressed (Erich Fromm: *Man For Himself*). ... These Neo-Freudian theories may have enlarged the scope of causes but at the price of eliminating the virtue of the Freud concept of the universality of the self-seeking or pleasure-seeking inclination of the self. Thus they capitulated to the errors of the Enlightenment and sought particular causes for universal phenomena. There are of course always specific causes for specific forms of self-regard or the will to power or human vanity. The self-regard of a German general, a Japanese abbot and an American go-getter have different historical causes. But it would be ill-advised to have a completely nominalistic attitude toward these phenomena and to assume that we could eliminate these forms of self-regard by progressively eliminating the specific causes of specific

forms of it.[16]

This paragraph reveals the very heart of Niebuhr's difficulty with many forms of psychotherapy, namely, they *offer a very specific and particular solution for a problem which is universal.* We will not be able to find specific, concrete, psychological *causes* of excessive self-regard because it is a universal problem. It may be exacerbated by our particular life circumstances, but it is not *completely caused* by those circumstances. Put directly, we cannot psychologically "fix" this undue self-focus.

> [T]he self is not in a position to absolve itself of blame because it regards its self-concern as ordinate. It is not in a position to judge. In any case it is inclined to judge itself leniently except in cases of religious self-awareness. Man, in short, is bound to have an uneasy conscience about his egoism, though he knows it to be a universal characteristic. He feels himself responsible, despite the inevitability of the corruption, because he always envisages a purer deed in prospect than it appears in retrospect. For in an honest respect the self will always be proved to have insinuated itself into the creative effort.[17]

In other words, as we have previously noted, Niebuhr is against any redemptive plan which attempts to reduce an ontological problem into a strictly psychological one. The specifics of each person's past can be worked through and to a large extent healed. The unique struggles with fear, guilt, obsession, and a host of other psychological problems can be largely resolved. But *the* predicament, the ontological anxiety built into the very structure of life, will serve as the breeding ground for more destructive behavior. We cannot turn our existential struggles into simple psychological or biological problems. They grow out of our capacity for self-transcendence.

Again, various forms of psychotherapy locate the primary human dilemma within a specific psychological process—unempathic parents, too much guilt, sibling rivalry, an enmeshed family, our dad's drinking, our mother's obsessive-compulsive habits, *ad infinitum.* These may indeed be contributing causes to the struggles of our lives. But turning the colossal problem of ontological anxiety and insecurity into highly specific, identifiable finite sources will not resolve the human dilemma. Psychology sometimes seems to suggest that if parents would only quit shaming their

---

[16]Niebuhr, "Human Creativity and Self-Concern in Freud," 271.
[17]Niebuhr, "Human Creativity and Self-Concern in Freud,' 273.

children we'd have perfectly balanced, loving kids; if we could simply build every child's self-esteem, the crime rate would completely drop; if we could only teach better communication skills, there would be no more violence. These are all worthwhile goals but, as we saw in the last chapter, they will not eliminate the excessive self-regard born out of our anxiety. Evil, then, cannot ultimately be explained by natural impulses which reason can tame. Neither can evil be ultimately explained by historical, personal, or social causes. We could bring in a never-ending litany of psychological, social, economic, and historical factors to account for why humanity is in the shape its in. But none of these will let us off the hook because we all—even those raised by self-esteem building parents, those raised with a surplus of wealth, those with an abundance of educational opportunities, and those with a high degree of family solidarity—will find ourselves caught up in an anxiety-triggered excessive self-regard.

Love and Self-Sacrifice

Given Freud's view of the human condition, he believed that the command-ment to love one's neighbor as oneself was psychologically impossible. Even more so did Freud believe the idea of loving a stranger or one's ene-my to be completely out of the question. Freudian scholar Ernest Wallwork makes the convincing point however, that Freud *did* believe in a mutual respect and certain reciprocity in our relationships.[18] Freud believed it would be far more realistic to say that instead of "loving our neighbors as ourselves" we should have instead been commanded to "love our neighbors as they love us." Any pretense of self-sacrificial love or *agape*, for Freud, is both unrealistic and dangerous. Freud would say that it is dangerous be-cause, as a naturalist, he believes it puts entirely too much pressure on a finite human being, pressure which will surely prompt a later revolt.

Niebuhr also holds a somewhat controversial view on the possibilities of *agape*. He would agree that all we can expect on a regular, consistent basis in finite human relationships is mutuality and respect, not agape. However, Niebuhr also believes that *agape* can occasionally break into historical existence and transform us. This self-sacrificial love is an ideal possibility even though it is not regularly practiced. It is a very important

---

[18]Ernest Wallwork, *Psychoanalysis and Ethics* (New Yaven CT: Yale University Press, 1991).

and meaningful goal for which to strive. Also, Niebuhr does not believe that agape is completely unlike mutuality and equal regard. Instead, it builds upon it. Agape does not repress or destroy mutuality in order to express itself. Self-sacrificial love can build on the energies of mutual love. Further, agape does *not* mean feeling a deep emotional connection or affection for everyone. It is here that Freud had a very different understanding of neighbor love than Niebuhr held. For Freud, neighbor love involves a warm and affectionate disposition whereas for Niebuhr it refers to a nonexploitive attitude of good will toward another.

Yet for Niebuhr, agape is necessary because mutual or reciprocal love cannot fulfill itself. The reason is that we can easily get caught up in calculating the level of reciprocity in our relationships. As long as reciprocity is in place, mutual love may not be too demanding. But what happens during those periods in which mutuality is not forthcoming? What happens when we feel as if this is the third time in a row that we've given of ourselves this week and there has been no return of our investment? It is here that self-sacrificial love can be injected to provide the additional strength we need. However, it is important to point out that this self-sacrificial love will eventually need to be balanced if resentment is not to occur. If self-sacrifice becomes a *permanent pattern* in a relationship, when in fact mutuality should govern the relationship, then the imbalance will lead to enormous difficulty. While I may be more sacrificial this month than you are, it may be your turn next month. In other words, the overall movement of our relationship needs to be toward reciprocal care and mutual love. A strict emphasis on continual self-sacrifice can be an easy set up for exploitation and oppression. It is no wonder that feminists and other minority groups have been very concerned about this emphasis. Like many other mid-twentieth century theologians, Niebuhr emphasized self-sacrifice as the primary remedy for self-exaltation. Yet for those who needed greater self-assertion, the message could easily be an obstacle.

Yet again, Niebuhr did not think self-sacrificial love was altogether different than mutual love. This is where he disagreed with theological ethicist Anders Nygren, who insisted on a radical distinction between *agape* and *eros*.[19] For Nygren, there is a strong break between concerns for the self and concerns for others. Much like Luther, Nygren believed that true

---

[19]For a fuller discussion of Niebuhr, Nygren, and Agape, see Browning and Cooper, *Religious Thought and the Modern Psychologies*, 130-43.

Christian love never comes from our own resources or natural energies. Instead, it comes strictly from God. In other words, it is completely unlike anything humanity can bring forth. We may be instruments through which divine love may flow, but this divine love will *not* build on human love.

Louis Janssens, on the other hand, argues that self-sacrificial love is not the final goal in human life.[20] Instead, the final goal is mutuality. In order to achieve this goal of mutuality, self-sacrificial must sometimes come to the rescue. Perhaps the other person, for a time, is not capable of being reciprocal. Yet again, this should not represent a permanent ideal. Self-sacrifice is a transitional ethic to help the larger goal of mutuality and reciprocity.

We must resist any notion of self-sacrificial love that robs us of dignity and eliminates our self-respect. There is a huge difference between meeting another's genuine needs and being exploited by them. There is no virtue in being someone's door mat. We should also resist being exploited because it reinforces that behavior in another person. In other words, it will make it more likely that they will also oppress others as well. It will become an unjust and unhealthy pattern which "works" for them.

Also, as we have seen, loving our neighbor does not mean that we have an equally deep affection for *all* people. We do not love all people in the same way emotionally. If we did, our love would not mean much. We what are called to do is offer an attitude of equal regard as we respect the person-hood of each individual we encounter and demonstrate a concern for their well-being. If everyone is my friend, no one is my friend. But that doesn't mean that I can't act in friendly ways even to those I do not know.

Summarizing Niebuhr's Estimation of Freud

In summary, then, Niebuhr appreciates Freud's genius and utilizes Freud's portrait of our estranged condition. He differed with Freud, however, on the belief that destructiveness is built into the core of our being. Freud was *right* about our fallen nature, but *wrong* about our essential nature. There is nothing about the structure of human existence which necessitates sin or destructiveness. Once again, Niebuhr's comment is basically the same to both Augustine and Freud: Sin does not have biological roots. Our proclivi-

---

[20]Louis Jannsens, "Norms and Priotites in a Love Ethics," *Louvain Studies* 6 (Spring 1977).

ties toward excessive self-regard and injustice toward our neighbors come from our so-called higher aspirations, not our brute instincts. In short, Niebuhr does not think Freud adequately considers the self-seeking nature of the *ego itself*. The id is obviously self-seeking and the superego can be quite self-centered. But Freud didn't expand much on the possibilities that the ego, too, could act in self-serving ways. As Niebuhr puts it, "The chief difficulty in the Freudian analysis of the self is that it is blind to the resources for both love and self-love at the very heights of human personality, rather than in a pleasure-seeking id."[21]

Self-Realization: Niebuhr and Carl Jung

One of the most abiding themes in Niebuhr's thought is the conviction that self-realization can never be reached if it is directly pursued. He describes this paradox of self-fulfillment:

> It is an obvious fact, which may be "empirically" observed, that the self does not fulfill itself most fully when self-realization is its conscious aim. In the same way happiness and virtue elude conscious striving. In any event, prudent calculation is not powerful enough to draw the self from itself as the center of its existence and to find a center beyond itself.[22]

Self-realization is a by-product, a secondary effect of a life committed to a larger purpose than the self. It is, in fact, quite self-defeating to make the pursuit of happiness the central goal of one's life. We are not designed to be our own end. Niebuhr points toward the frustration which often accompanies the direct pursuit of self-fulfillment: "Most irksome of all, perhaps, is the discovery that the chief prizes in life do not come primarily by planning. Whether it is happiness or self-realization, love or virtue, that we seek, we find that it is less likely to come as a result of direct efforts than as a by-product of devotion to something else.[23] We find ourselves by losing ourselves, as Jesus reminded us. We must look beyond the clamoring demands of self-regard and throw ourselves into a life of love and service. Stated more strongly, the self is always tempted to destroy itself because it seeks itself too narrowly. This consuming inward focus has the ironic effect

---

[21]Quoted in Bingham, *Courage to Change*, 93.

[22]Reinhold Niebuhr, *The Self and the Dramas of History* (New York: Scribner's, 1955) 32.

[23]Quoted in Bigham, *Courage to Change*, 38.

of not leading to self-clarity. Like the runner who is doing well until he becomes preoccupied with his feet, the self is not intended to fixate on itself.

This theme of dying to the self and rising again to a new life is expressed by Niebuhr this way: "Therefore the death and resurrection of Christ is felt to be symbolic of the dying of self to its narrow self, that it may truly live."[24] This comment sounds very similar to Jung's notion of dying to the ego in the service of the larger Self. The small, self-preoccupying focus of the ego will sabotage the spiritual journey. For Jung this process often does not happen until the second half of life. The preoccupations of the ego during the first half of life eventually give way to a much larger focus. This death to the ego, however, is often a painful one.

For Jung, then, there is an important difference between the ego and the "Self." [25]The ego refers to the conscious part of personality, the sense of "I" which chooses particular actions. It is the conscious agency of the personality and it is sustained through memory. The "Self," on the other hand, includes but goes beyond, the ego. The Self refers to everything within the entire psyche, both conscious and unconscious. For Jung, the ego is concerned with appearance, advancement, and control of the external world. In order to function in the social world, it wears a mask, which Jung called the persona. There is nothing wrong with wearing this persona *as long as one realizes that he or she is wearing a persona*. The problem comes when we believe that the persona is all that we are. We so identify with this social mask that we think it describes our entire being. As we overidentify with the pesona, we repress and split off those parts of ourselves which do not match this public image. Those feelings, thoughts, or experiences which do not match the standards of the persona's expectations are pushed underground. We attempt to better than we are. In fact, we attempt to be better than we can possibly be. Those rejected parts of our experience which do not match the ideals of the ego are called the "shadow." Jung calls the shadow "the negative side of the personality, the sum of all those unpleasant qualities we like to hide, together with the insufficiently developed functions aand the content of the personal unconscious."[26] In spite of the fact that parts of our experience are rejected and thrown into the storage bin of

---

[24]Quoted in Bingham, *Courage to Change*, 325.

[25]Carl Jung, *The Undiscovered Self* (New York: Signet, 2006).

[26]Carl Jung, *Collected Works*, vol. 2 (Princeton NJ: Princeton University Press, 1969).

the shadow, they stay with us. In fact, they can rise up and sabotage us at vulnerable moments. The story of the shadow is the story of the perils and pitfalls of self-rejection. In other words, we need to very careful about what we refuse to own. It may retreat, but we are hardly "done with it."

Jung believed that the shadow explains a great deal of our hatred toward others. Cut off from our own darker inclinations, we are particularly prone to see these inclinations in others and go on the attack. In other words, we deny these qualities in ourselves, see evidence of them in others—which reminds us of ourselves—then attack the projected image. Put simply, others *carry our shadows*. They form this valuable task of keeping our attention focused on *their* evil and not our own. A fixation on judging and ridiculing others becomes a handy escape from confronting our own demons. Little do we realize that these "sinners" around us are holding up mirrors and we are really seeing ourselves. In fact, if we ceased to judge them, we might be forced to turn our attention back to ourselves.[27]

Niebuhr would clearly agree with Jung that good and evil are not simply opposite forces which are quite separable and distinguishable from each other. They are intertwined within every individual as well as intertwined in history. While he doesn't use the Jungian language of a "shadow," Niebuhr clearly indicates that there is a dark side to even the most righteous people. In fact, Niebuhr is perpetually suspicious of people who appear too righteous. His rigorous condemnation of self-righteousness is renown. Niebuhr is fond of Mark 2:15-18:

> And as he sat at a table in his house, many tax collectors and sinners were sitting with Jesus and his disciples; for there were many who followed him. And the scribes of the Pharisees, when they saw that he was eating with sinners and tax collectors, said to his disciples, "Why does he eat with tax collectors and sinners?" And when Jesus heard it, he said to them, "Those who are well have no need of a physician, but those who are sick; I came not to call the righteous, but sinners." (RSV)

For Niebuhr, when Jesus refers to those who are "well" or "whole," he means people who *think* they are well rather than people who are actually well.[28] These are people who see no need for repentance. Yet for Niebuhr,

---

[27]For a fuller discussion of Jung's view of evil and its connection to Christian theology, see my *Dimensions of Evil: Contemporary Perspectives*, chap. 3.

[28]Niebuhr, "Christian Revelation and Human Hope. Sermon on Mark 2:15-19,"

of course, everyone is in dire need of grace and repentance. There is no final vindication through anyone's righteousness. Instead, the final triumph comes through God's mercy. This is the central symbol of the cross, namely, that at the point where we may hope to see our own righteousness triumph, it is redeemed only by God's mercy. As we have already seen, Niebuhr spent a lifetime pointing toward the less obvious forms of sin, the sins of a self-righteous demeanor which claimed to be above sin. For Niebuhr, humility plus God's mercy equals transformation. Grace is both forgiveness and power. It is precisely this awareness of our own forgiveness which allows us to forgive others in a noncondescending manner. Thus, Jung and Niebuhr both share a suspicion about those who appear to be "a little *too* good." Niebuhr reclaims the Lutheran position that we are always saint and sinner. We may be a forgiven sinner but we are clearly a sinner. In fact, in making this important point, some have wondered whether Niebuhr has ignored altogether the important issue of the traditional doctrine of "sanctification." Some argue that Niebuhr so abhors self-righteousness and religious pretense, that he nearly eliminates any emphasis on spiritual development. Because this development often comes accompanied by pride, Niebuhr negates it. Thus, it may not be completely without warrant that Niebuhr is accused of omitting any emphasis on the Holy Spirit.[29] His disdain for any notion of perfectionism may make him somewhat dismissive of an emphasis on spiritual development.

A key difference between Niebuhr and Jung, however, is that Niebuhr refuses to ontologize evil. It is not an essential part of the human condition and it is certainly not an essential part of the Divine. Jung rather famously believed that evil had ontological status as a permanent part of being. In fact, evil is even part of the Godhead. We have polarized good and evil in Christianity by insisting on the radical difference, symbolically speaking, between God and Satan. For Jung, Satan is simply God's shadow, the alienated part of the Divine. Jung is ultimately a monist who believes that these polarities in life must be integrated. In this sense, he could not possibly be further away from Freud, who, as we have seen, believed in two

---

Reinhold Niebuhr Audio Tape Collection / Reinhold Niebuhr Compact Disc Collection, Union Theological Seminary in Virginia, per Ann Knox <aknox@union-psce.edu>.

[29]Rachel Hadley King, *The Omission of the Holy Spirit from Reinhold Niebuhr's Theology* (New York: Philosophical Library, 1964).

competing forces which will always be at war. By symbolically speaking of a Divine quartet (Father, Son, Holy Spirit, and Satan) instead of a trinity, Jung points toward the need for God's shadow to be integrated within the Divine life. Thus, evil is a necessary part of being. In fact, it only appears to us as evil because it is cut off from Divine communion. For Jung, once integration has occurred, either personally or cosmically, evil will be seen as a necessary polarity to achieve balance.

Yet while Jung locates evil as an eternal fixture within being, Niebuhr insists that evil is a corruption, and therefore not necessary. As we have seen, Niebuhr denies any perspective which even remotely insinuates that evil is a necessary part of creation. Thus, while Niebuhr would appreciate Jung's discussion of self-realization as going beyond the needs of the ego, and would further affirm Jung's emphasis on the shadow in even the "purest" behavior, he would differ with Jung's ultimate monism in which evil is part of the Divine.

Niebuhr and Karen Horney

Like Niebuhr, psychoanalyst Karen Horney's view of the self begins with anxiety. By basic anxiety, Horney means "the feeling a child has of being isolated and helpless in a potentially hostile world."[30] She also agrees with Niebuhr that while this anxiety is not itself destructive, it is the breeding ground for neurosis, or what Niebuhr calls sin. Horney lists some of the various factors which can easily arouse excessive anxiety:

> A wide range of adverse factors can produce this insecurity in a child: direct or indirect domination, indifference, erratic behavior, lack of respect for the child's individual needs, lack of real guidance, disparaging attitudes, too much admiration or the absence of it, lack of reliable warmth, having to take sides in parental disagreements, too much or too little responsibility, overprotection, isolation from other children, injustice, discrimination, unkept promises, hostile atmosphere, and so on and so on.[31]

In an effort to deal with this basic anxiety, a child frequently develops one of these patterns of relating to others—patterns which attempt to reduce anxiety and minimize threat in relationships. These three patterns or "neurotic trends," as Horney calls them, are a major part of her personality

---

[30]Karen Horney, *Our Inner Conflicts* (New York: W. W. Norton, 1945) 41.
[31]Horney, *Our Inner Conflicts*, 41.

theory. They offer enormous insight into interpersonal dynamics and they also richly illustrate Nieubuhr's discussion of both pride and sensuality.

The first movement is what Horney frequently calls "moving against others." This pattern involves self-expansion and is quite similar to Niebuhr's classic description of pride. This trend emerges as persons attempts to defeat anxiety by controlling, conquering, and dominating everything around them. This trend is based on an exaggerated need to master everything in life. A premium is placed on will power and intelligence. The underlying fear which drives this will to power is a sense of helplessness. All self-doubt, all insecurity, and all fragility must be eliminated. In short, this is an attempt to short-circuit finitude. All failures must be ignored. Self-expansive types, according to Horney, are proud that they cannot be fooled, conned, or manipulated. This self-expansive approach manifests itself in narcissism, perfectionism, and entitlement claims. Because these individuals always need to be the best at everything they do, they are extremely competitive and jealous of anyone whose abilities seem to challenge their own. There is often a desire to intimidate others into submission. Violent rage frequently accompanies any thought of being surpassed. These individuals have a profound insensitivity toward others, and in some cases, a sadistic desire to humiliate them. They demand to have their own needs met while disregarding the needs of others. Horney describes this type of person:

> He feels entitled for instance to the unabridged expression of his unfavorable observations and criticisms but feels equally entitled to never be criticized himself. He is entitled to decide how often or how seldom to see a friend and what to do with the time spent together. Conversely, he also is entitled not to have others express any expectations or objections on this score.[32]

There is very little, if any, consciousness about imposing on others or demanding too much of them. Again, one is entitled.

Not only do the "moving against others" people lack an understanding of the unconscious, they in fact will probably ridicule and "put down" the very notion of the unconscious. The reason for this negative view of the unconscious is quite simple: If they admitted the unconscious elements in their own actions, they would suddenly feel out of control. Their self-

---

[32]Karen Horney, *Neurosis and Human Growth* (New York: W. W. Norton, 1950) 200.

mastery would be called into question as they dealt with the frightening possibility that their behavior may be influenced by processes outside of their conscious control. Thus, they are dismissive of references to the unconscious as well as suspicious of conversations about their "inner" world. Most "moving against" types are not fans of psychology. And if they are attracted to psychology, their interest is in "using" it to better manipulate and control others.

There is little doubt that Horney's description of this inflated person matches very well Niebuhr's discussion of pride. Both thinkers believe that in an attempt to get rid of anxiety, individuals inflate themselves and become interpersonally destructive. Whether we call it excessive self-regard or neurotic pride, the profile seems the same.

While the self-expansive movement is one interpersonal problem, the self-effacing solution to anxiety is another. Horney calls this the "moving toward" inclination. Rather than domination, the focus in this interpersonal movement is on radical accommodation. Persons must win the affection and approval of others if conflict is to be avoided. Compliance becomes the magic ingredient to interpersonal peace. Any form of self-assertion, initiative, or ambition must be prohibited because it creates anxiety about how persons might get along with others. Rather than pursuing self-expansion, these individuals avoid it. Full of constant apologies, they are always preoccupied with what others want. As Horney puts it on several occasions, their "sense of gravity" seems to be in others rather than themselves. This is an early description of what many in the 1980s began to call "codependency." It often involves the worship of another while ignoring oneself. Speaking up about legitimate rights is prohibited because of a fear of seeming "selfish." Any sign of ambition is pushed aside because it must mean that one doesn't appreciate what one already has. As Horney likes to put it, these persons choose to live their lives within "narrow borders." They often have difficulty acknowledging any sense of accomplishment

The fear of conflict drives these "moving toward" types to a subordinate position. They "give in" easily to avoid any serious difference of disagreement. They are more than ready to admit mistakes and claim that most things are their fault. As Horney puts it:

> Summarizing all this, we could say that there are taboos on all that is presumptuous, selfish, and aggressive. If we realize in detail the scope covered by the taboos, they constitute a crippling check on the person's expansion, his capacity for fighting and for defending himself, his self-interest—on anything

that might accrue to his growth or self-esteem. The taboos and self-minimizing constitute a *shrinking process.* . . . [33]

Self-effacing persons will often criticize themselves before anyone else has a chance to criticize them. This takes some of the pain out of being criticized by others. They also may achieve from others what they really want—sympathetic assurance.

But why would anyone engage in this peace-at-all-costs pattern of behavior? The primary reason is that these individuals are so desperate for the approval and acceptance of others. But then we might ask why they so desperately need the approval and acceptance of others. And the answer appears to be that their anxiety leaves them feeling empty inside, unable to achieve any sense of self-adequacy apart from "borrowing" acceptance from others. The affirmation of others becomes a temporary "fix" for the desert of one's own emptiness.

This excessive need for approval and peace leaves the "moving toward" person with an inability to be discriminating about people. They compulsively need the approval of *everyone*. Hence, they can never say "no" to a person, no matter how much that person may gobble up their time, attention, or resources.

> On the surface it looks as though he had an unshakable faith in the essential goodness of humanity. And it is true that he is more open, more sensitive, to likeable qualities in others. But the compulsiveness of his expectations makes it impossible for him to be discriminating. He cannot as a rule distinguish between genuine friendliness and its many counterfeits. He is too easily bribed by any show of warmth or interest. In addition, his inner dictates tell him that he *should* like everybody, that he *should* not be suspicious. Finally, his fear of antagonism and possible fights makes him overlook, discard, minimize, or explain away such traits as lying, crookedness, exploiting, cruelty, or treachery. [34]

Even when the exploitive, deceitful, and manipulative behavior of others is pointed out, the self-effacing person will often say that they really didn't mean it. Their intentions were pure even if their behavior was not. They *need* to believe that no one is intentionally malicious. Why? Because their own source of approval and acceptance comes from others. They have a *vested interest* in seeing others in a positive light. Thus they whitewash

---

[33] Horney, *Neurosis and Human Growth*, 219.
[34] Horney, *Neurosis and Human Growth*, 226.

other people in order to believe they can get an "approval fix" from them. Put another way, if other people are incapable of offering them acceptance and approval, then their *entire solution* to the anxiety problem is sabotaged. Others must be seen as basically "good"; otherwise, the approval supply would be challenged and cut off.

As one might easily guess, a huge part of this "moving toward others" solution is finding a partner who will take over one's life. The self-effacing person needs someone to worship. The idea of being alone is unbearable. Horney provides a vivid characterization of a woman who is ready to worship a partner.

> The first characteristic to strike us is such a woman's total absorption in the relationship. The partner becomes the sole center of her existence. Everything revolves around him. Her mood depends upon whether his attitude toward her is more positive or negative. She does not dare make any plans lest she might miss a call or an evening with him. Her endeavors are directed toward measuring up to what she feels he expects. She has but one fear—that of antagonizing and losing him. Conversely her other interests subside. Her work, unless connected with him, becomes comparatively meaningless. This may even be true of professional work otherwise dear to her heart, or productive work in which she has accomplished things.[35]

There is a strong need here to remain inconspicuous and remain in second place. Any hint of surpassing one's partner is desperately denied. Modesty is the superior quality above everything else. Humility is the goal as all arrogance must be crushed.

It is not hard to guess that self-effacing persons often get together with self-expanding types. One of the reasons, according to Horney, is that while self-mastery is denied in self-effacing individuals, they secretly admire it in others. Blocked from it in their own lives, they enjoy it vicariously through their partners. They are, in a sense, power voyeurs. Also, they like strong and dominating individuals because any hint of weakness or insecurity in others reminds them of themselves. The idea of being the stronger one in the relationship is very frightening. Their own repressed desire for power and control pushes them toward an obsession of it in others.

Horney's description of a self-effacing person matches Niebuhr's portrayal of one form of sensuality, namely, the person who avoids the anxiety

---

[35]Horney, *Neurosis and Human Growth*, 247-48.

of his or her own life by making a god of another person. The other person replaces God as the center and source of one's life. Yet what is even more interesting is Horney's conviction, again similar to Niebuhr's, that there is pride lurking behind this seemingly pitiful self-effacing solution. While the self-effacing solution may at first appear to involve enormous low self-esteem and a self-depreciative attitude, there is an underlying "pride system" at work. This pride system demands that one not be like other people. In other words, one's standards must be above the traffic of ordinary human behavior. Other people may become angry or agitated in the face of insensitivities and abuse, but one is "above" that selfish reaction. Other people may strike back in protest, but they do not share one's own exalted standard of patience. This sense of humility actually becomes a sense of pride. While it may sound dreadful to say this to a person who seems to lack self-esteem, it might be helpful to ask: "Just who do you think you are?" In other words, these more-than-human demands for shrinking self-concern may in fact be built on a pride system which *really believes* one can achieve a constant practice of pure *agape*. While self-effacing persons understand that *others* cannot achieve this exalted standard and does not expect it of them, they demand it of themselves. But this very demand is based on a form of pride, namely, a pride that one *should* be able to accomplish what no one else can. This is the insidiousness of pride: When we work so hard at a more-than-human elimination of self-regard, we are unconsciously proud of how selfless we are. For Horney, it is these inner dictates about selflessness *which are themselves* full of neurotic pride.

The third movement described by Horney is "moving away from others." This refers to a tendency to resolve the anxiety of life by self-resignation. It is an attitude of detachment or aloofness. Self-sufficiency is the primary goal in this movement because the idea of needing others creates enormous anxiety. Being close to others also brings up fears of engulfment and the loss of freedom. In order to escape this interpersonal imprisonment, distance and separateness is sought.

> Where the compliant type looks at his fellow man with the silent question, "Will he like me?"—and the aggressive type wants to know, "How strong an adversary is he?" or "Can he be useful to me?"—the detached person's first concern is, "Will he interfere with me? Will he want to influence me or will he

leave me alone?"[36]

Horney makes an important distinction between constructive and compulsive resignation. Constructive resignation wisely recognizes that some of our ambitions may be foolish or impossible. But compulsive resignation gives up appropriate and important ambitions. It attempts to solve the anxiety problem by wanting nothing, having no expectations, and therefore never being disappointed by life. Resigned persons become spectators of life rather than participants. Horney suggests that these individuals are excellent at finding reasons for *not* doing things. Goal-oriented behavior is too much of a "bother." Again, the secret of happiness is to wish for very little. They often feel entitled to a life of painless and effortless peace. Quite frankly, they'd rather simply be left alone. Relationships, themselves, involve too much energy. And they are hypersensitive to pressure or coercion coming from others. Horney describes the "moving away" person when she says that "he feels entitled to having others not intrude upon his privacy, to having them not expect anything of him or bother him, to be exempt from having to make a living and from responsibilities."[37]

This self-resignation tendency looks a lot like the traditional deadly sin of sloth. Thus, here too, Horney provides a helpful description for Niebuhr's understanding of self-escape. Self-resignation involves pulling back from the turmoil and possible frustration of selfhood. It is the opposite of "the courage to be." It retreats from the ambiguities of life by denying life itself.

Earlier, I mentioned that the problem of egoism (self-preoccupation) is deeper for Niebuhr than the problem of egotism (self-exaltation). This is also true of Horney. She believes that in *all three movements* to reduce anxiety a self-preoccupation emerges. Though lengthy, her comment on the nature of egocentricity is worth quoting:

> To begin with, the pride system removes the neurotic from others by making him *egocentric*. To avoid misunderstandings: by egocentricity I do not mean selfishness or egotism in the sense of considering merely one's own advantage. The neurotic may be callously selfish or too unselfish—there is nothing in this regard that is characteristic for all neuroses. But he is always egocentric in the sense of being wrapped up in himself. This need not be apparent on the

---

[36]Horney, *Our Inner Conflicts*, 80-81.
[37]Horney, *Neurosis and Human Growth*, 271.

surface—he may be a lone wolf or live for and through others. Nevertheless he lives in any case by his private religion (his idealized image), abides by his own laws (his shoulds), within the barbed-wire fence of his own pride and with his guards to protect him against dangers from within and without. As a result he not only becomes more isolated emotionally but it also becomes more difficult for him to see other people as individuals in their own right, different from himself. They are subordinated to his prime concern: himself.[38]

For Horney, it is impossible to be attentive toward others when we cannot escape our own self-fixation. We may need to be admired, to be approved, to avoid conflict, to dominate others, or to be left alone. But our need, like a toothache, controls our attention and turns it back on ourselves. Thus, once again, *self-absorption is broader than self-inflation.*

Niebuhrian pride is also very similar to what Horney's frequently calls the "search for glory." The search for glory involves a quest to reach for what is beyond the realm of human possibility. As Horney puts it, "all the drives for glory have in common the reaching out for greater knowledge, wisdom, virtue, or powers than are given to human beings; they all aim at the *absolute*, the unlimited, the infinite."[39] Our inability to accept our finitude pushes us toward a restless attempt to be the god of our own life. This search for glory always involves a refusal to recognize our limits. Niebuhr would say that it is the story of the Garden of Eden all over again. Note how Horney's biographer, Bernard Paris, puts this:

> Horney does not see the search for glory, the quest for the absolute, or the need to be godlike as essential ingredients of human nature. Because we have the ability to imagine and plan, we are always reaching beyond ourselves. . . . For Freud our condition is tragic because the requirements for survival—civilization—prohibit that full and immediate gratification of instinct which is the only source of true happiness. For Horney tragedy is not inherent in the human condition, but our lives become tragic when "under pressures of distress" we try to transcend our condition by reaching out "for the ultimate and the infinite" and in the process destroy the potentialities we actually possess and condemn ourselves to self-hate.[40]

---

[38]Horney, *Neurosis and Human Growth*, 291-92.

[39]Horney, *Neurosis and Human Growth*, 34.

[40]Bernard Paris, *Karen Horney: A Psychoanalyst's Search for Self-Understanding* (New Haven CT: Yale University Press, 1994) 204.

It is crucial to note the similarities here between Horney's and Niebuhr's views of Freud. It is almost as if Horney is saying that "neurosis is inevitable but not necessary." We are not hardwired for destructive disturbance as Freud suggests. Horney argues that we do not *have* to engage in a search for glory, develop an idealized self, or fall into one of the neurotic patterns in an attempt to conquer anxiety. And yet we seem to.

It is important, here, however, to mention a key difference between Horney and Niebuhr. Horney seems to hold onto the possibility that with the right kind of psychological environment, we can rise above neurotic pride. In that sense, she locates the source of anxiety in something other than human freedom. Thus, she, like Carl Rogers, does not adequately highlight the significance of ontological anxiety, the anxiety which is simply part of the human condition and which always tempts persons toward idolatry. As we have seen, if one makes the source of anxiety a problem in one's psychosocial context, then the next step is to "fix' that problem and thus eliminate anxiety. For Niebuhr, as for Tillich and Rollo May, this will never work. Self-conscious finitude brings with it the temptation to act with excessive self-regard. Thus, Horney falls into the same utopianism as does Erich Fromm. The idea that we can cure an ontological problem with a psychological mechanism is for Niebuhr quite impossible. So while there are many areas of similarity between them, Niebuhr and Horney do not stand in agreement on the prognosis for curing ontological anxiety. For Niebuhr, ontological anxiety can only be healed by a trust in God and life. Ontological anxiety is primarily a theological problem rather than a psychological one. Wanting to move beyond a "creaturely" status, we reach toward godhood. This produces neurotic pride but it doesn't produce genuine self-confidence. Never satisfied with our humanness and always attempting to outsmart the problem of anxiety, we become excessively preoccupied with self. This is the great enemy of love of God and neighbor.

Niebuhr and Erich Fromm

Since the publication of his *Man for Himself: An Inquiry into the Psychology of Ethics* in 1947, Erich Fromm has emphasized the importance of self-love in mental health.[41] Unlike Freud, who argued that self-love is the great

---

[41]Erich Fromm, *Man for Himself: An Inquiry into the Psychology of Ethics* (New York: Holt, Rinehart, and Winston, 1947).

obstacle to loving others, Fromm believed that self-love is legitimate and necessary. Freud believed that human beings only have a certain amount of libido, and if we love ourselves, we will have nothing left for others. While primary narcissism or a primitive form of self-love is appropriate for early life, we should move outside of this self-absorption and learn to relate to others. In short, self-love eliminates object love. In fact, as we shall see in the next chapter, Freud virtually gave up on the possibility of psycho-analyzing narcissists. Because narcissists have not adequately developed genuine relationships with people outside themselves, they have nothing to transfer in the psychoanalytic session. Without transference, there can be no psychoanalytic cure.

Yet Fromm sees this very differently. Rather than viewing self-love as robbing the libidinous energy to love others, Fromm believes that the love of others can spill over from self-love. Self-love does not drain our love tank; in fact, it fills it up and allows us to reach out to others as well. Rather than creating a deficiency, self-love instead creates a surplus—a surplus we can then share with others. There is no "love shortage" in Fromm's framework. Love perpetuates itself and allows for the possibility of loving others. In fact, Fromm argues that a lack of self-love, even a self-hatred, *makes the love of others impossible.*

Even a casual glance at Fromm's influential book, *Escape from Freedom* will reveal that Fromm has very little use for the Protestant reformers, Luther and Calvin.[42] In fact Fromm calls believes that both Luther and Calvin are two of the biggest self-haters in human history. Here is his description:

> Luther and Calvin portray this all-pervading hostility. Not only n the sense that these two men, personally, belonged to the ranks of the greatest haters among the leading figures of history, certainly among religious leaders; but, which is most important, in the sense that their doctrines were colored by this hostility and could only appeal to a group itself driven by an intense, repressed hostility.[43]

This is quite an indictment. Niebuhr would agree with Fromm that the Protestant reformers went too far in their denunciation of human goodness.

---

[42]Erich Fromm, *Escape from Freedom* (New York: Avon Books, 1941) esp. chap. 3.

[43]Fromm, *Escape From Freedom*, 115.

In an effort to demonstrate the self's inability to secure itself, the Reformers exaggerated the extent of our wickedness. Yet Fromm goes so far as to suggest that the Protestant reformers—the very thinkers who have greatly influenced Niebuhr, contribute to a sadomasochistic understanding of God. Sounding much like the nineteenth-century thinker, Feuerbach, Fromm believes that both Luther and Calvin portray God as "everything" while humanity is "nothing." Note the following two statements, the first by Feuerbach and the second by Fromm. In *The Essence of Christianity*, Feuerbach says:

> To enrich God, man must become poor; that God may be all, man must be nothing. But he desires to be nothing in himself, because what he takes from himself is not lost to him since it is preserved in God. . . . In brief, man in relation to God denies his knowledge, his own thoughts that he may place them in God. Man gives up his personality. . . . He denies human dignity, the human ego; but in return God is to him a selfish, egotistical being, who in all things seeks only himself, his own honor, his own ends. . . . His God is the very beginning of egotism.[44]

And then in his Terry Lectures at Yale, Fromm asserts:

> The more perfect God becomes, the more imperfect man becomes. He *projects* the best he has onto God and thus impoverishes himself. Now God has all love, all wisdom, all justice—and man is deprived of these qualities, he is empty and poor. He had begun with the feeling of smallness, but he now has become completely powerless and without strength; all his powers have been projected onto God. This mechanism of projection is the very same which can be observed in interpersonal relationships of a masochistic, submissive character, where one person is awed by another and attributes his own powers and aspirations to the other person. It is the same mechanism that makes people endow the leaders with of even the most inhuman systems with qualities of superwisdom and kindness.[45]

For both Feuerbach and Fromm, humanity continues to alienate itself by creating God and projecting all of its good qualities onto this Divine image. Humanity then has only the negative, "leftover" qualities while all

---

[44]Ludwig Feuerbach, *The Essence of Christianity*, trans. George Eliot (New York: Harper & Brothers, 1957) 26-27, 30.

[45]Erich Fromm, *Psychoanalysis and Religion* (New York: Bantam, 1967; orig., 1950) 48-49.

virtues are projected onto God. In order for humanity to reclaim these positive qualities, the idea of God must be abandoned. Yet this projection
process is very subtle; in fact, human beings do it unconsciously. But the
result is self-alienation.

Thus, for Feuerbach and Fromm, there is a direct correlation between
an idealization of God and this debasement of humanity. A masochistic religious person submits to an all-powerful and authoritarian God, and by so
doing, devalues him/herself. In order to maintain this awesome "goodness"
of God, humanity is left with nothing.[46] Further, the conviction that our
efforts are utterly incapable of pleasing God promotes even more self-
hatred.

The theological notion of predestination, for instance, is designed, especially by Calvin, to generate a feeling of human powerlessness and deep
insignificance.[47] As Fromm puts it, "Calvin's God, in spite of all attempts
to preserve the idea of God's justice and love, has all the features of a tyrant
without any quality of love or even justice."[48] In fact, Fromm makes what
is for many an outrageous suggestion, namely, that this division of the elect
and the damned was a precursor to the later Nazi separation of the elite class
from the "vermin."[49] If we hold that God himself has decided that certain
people are destined for damnation while others are not, then perhaps
Hitler's "final solution" does not look so deplorable. For Fromm, the
psychological motivation of Calvin's double predestination is quite simple:
Calvin had a deep contempt for other human beings. Surely no loving
person could seriously entertain such a diabolical view of God.

J. Stanley Glen seems very close to Niebuhr when he questions this
Feuerbach/Fromm psychological image of a weak and pitiful human
passively submitting to an authoritarian God. As he puts it:

> Indeed, the picture of the frail, weak, timid, lonely little man quivering in fear
> of the big, booming world around him and of the forces of nature that add to
> the threat of the world has been overdone in psychological criticisms of
> religion. Instead, the emphasis is on the strength of man, or more correctly,
> upon what he presumes his strength to be and can accomplish. It concerns his

---

[46]Erich Fromm, *Escape from Freedom* (New York: Avon, 1941) 115-16.

[47]J. Stanley Glen, *Erich Fromm: A Protestant Critique* (Philadelphia:
Westminster, 1966) 56.

[48]Fromm, *Escape from Freedom*, 107.

[49]Fromm, *Escape from Freedom*, 81-122.

presumption respecting his gifts, powers, achievements, and ambitions—his glory in himself and in his world. The emphasis is not so much upon the childish world as upon the adult world; not so much upon the primitive world as upon the civilized, sophisticated world. The problem is undoubtedly that of man's movement *away* from God—his *escape from* God.[50]

Niebuhr would quickly add that as we survey human experience we find humanity dealing with its fragile, existential anxiety with enormous pretense and self-sufficiency. Rather humbling ourselves before some humanly constructed Deity, we are much more inclined to *take on the role of Deity ourselves*. Rather than pathetically crawling toward a God we think we need, our greater inclination is to either deify our own interests or arrogantly attach ourselves to the God and self-righteously look down on others.

Glen uses the example of Alcoholics Anonymous as an example of how "turning our lives over to a power greater than ourselves" is not necessarily sadomasochistic.[51] In fact, the paradox is that it can be empowering. Many individuals recovering from chemical dependency have reported that as they trust a "higher power" and seek to align themselves with a larger spiritual direction in their lives, *they gain, rather than lose, freedom*. By recognizing one's powerlessness over alcohol, one is able to obtain a sense of power. The passage through brokenness or "hitting bottom" is a necessary part of moving toward new strength. Niebuhr, whose famous serenity prayer is used at the beginning of every A. A. meeting, would certainly concur.

Again, Niebuhr agrees that the Reformers overstated the extent of human depravity. Perhaps they overemphasized the futility of human efforts in an attempt to combat the notion that our will power, without the assistance of Divine mercy and grace, is not enough. Niebuhr is certainly not as "down on human efforts" as Fromm believed the Reformers were. Yet he would certainly agree with Tillich that Fromm's utopian hopes of humanity healing its own ills is as naïve as Marx's humanistic eschatology.[52]

Also, Niebuhr, in a review of Fromm's *Man for Himself*, argues the

---

[50]Glen, *Erich Fromm: A Protestant Critique*, 134.

[51]Glen, *Erich Fromm: A Protestant Critique*, 153-54.

[52]For a discussion of Tillich's critique of Fromm, see my *Paul Tillich and Psychology: Historic and Contemporary Explorations in Theology, Psychotherapy, and Ethics* (Macon GA: Mercer University Press, 2006) esp. chap. 3.

following: "From the Christian standpoint the self-hatred which is supposed to make love impossible is actually the consequence of a too anxious pre-occupation with self."[53] In other words, self-hatred is an outgrowth of self-obsession. For Niebuhr, we excessively regard the very self we hate. Out of anxiety, we are giving the self undue attention and missing the point of life. Self-hatred emerges from an anxious preoccupation with our finitude. Even if we hate, we are still gazing too long at a mirror of ourselves. Thus, for Niebuhr, *even self-hate emerges from excessive self-regard.* The point of life is to live, not to become permanently preoccupied with ourselves. Self-hatred easily becomes an inverted form of pride and undue focus. Whether we love or hate the image of ourselves, the point is that it is preoccupying us and robbing us of the joys of connecting with others and God.

It is important to come back many tines to this central Niebuhrian thesis: Self-preoccupation narrows, limits, and impoverishes human life. It is never fulfilling. It is *not* that Niebuhr is against self-esteem; indeed, that would warrant severe criticism from the psychological community. Instead, Niebuhr is against self-obsession, excessive self-regard, or undue self-focus. This may take the form of self-inflation or self-hatred. But the point is that we are spending far too much time and energy preoccupied with ourselves. We are simply not designed to turn all this attention back on ourselves. Our fulfillment is in facing outward, connecting with others, and engaging a purpose larger than the self. Self-preoccupation is always the great enemy of self-fulfillment. Niebuhr puts it this way:

> Actually both admonitions, that the self ought to love itself and that the self ought to love others are spiritually impotent. An insecure and impoverished self is not made secure by the admonition to be concerned for itself: for an excessive concern for its security is the cause of the impoverishment. Nor is it made secure by the admonition to love others because that is precisely what it can not do because of its anxiety about itself. That is why a profound religion has always insisted that the self can not be cured by law but only by grace; and also why the profoundest forms of the Christian faith regard this preoccupation as not fully curable and therefore requiring another kind of grace: that of forgiveness.[54]

---

[53]Reinhold Niebuhr, review of *Man For Himself, Christianity and Society* 13/2 (Spring 1948): 27.

[54]Niebuhr, review of *Man for Himself*, 27-28.

Here, Niebuhr sounds like a very astute psychologist, one who recognizes that both poles of narcissism (grandiosity and self-hatred) emerge out of an excessive self-fixation. Whether we love ourselves inordinately or hate ourselves intensely, the underlying factor is a preoccupation with self, a preoccupation which robs us of the joys of living.

Summary

In summary, then, it is fair to say that Niebuhr took an appreciative but critical stance toward the psycholoanalytic tradition. He greatly appreciated Freud's vivid portrayal of the unconscious processes which frequently control our so-called "pure" rationality. He further believed that Freud's elaborations on the way the mind works to protect itself from reality offer a new language for the Judeo-Christian understanding of excessive self-regard. Yet while respecting Freud's genius, Niebuhr nevertheless believed that Freud made a fundamental error when he located the source of human destructiveness in our biological makeup. Put simply, he didn't believe we inherit a natural death instinct. Instead, destructive behavior arises from the mishandling of our freedom in the face of anxiety.

Niebuhr also holds an appreciation for Jung's refusal to divide the world into "us" and "them" categories. Jung's emphasis on the power of the shadow is a helpful reminder of the dangers of self-righteousness. It is also a restatement of the fact that we are always saint *and* sinner. Like Jung, Niebuhr was suspicious of individuals whose piety seemed "too good to be true." Niebuhr would further appreciate Jung's understanding that self-realization must always go beyond the parameters of the individual ego. In fact, he would agree with Jung that the concerns of the ego often sabotage the deeper journey of the self. Yet, as we have seen, Niebuhr would not agree with Jung's tendency to "ontologize" evil, and therefore make it a fundamental part of reality, including God. While Niebuhr encouraged us to look long and hard at the evil in our own hearts, he also exhorted us to combat the injustice and evil in the world around us. Any notion that evil is somehow necessary or part of an intricate part of the cosmic story would be rejected.

Niebuhr's work, at times, seems amazingly similar to Karen Horney's insights concerning the relationship between pride and self-contempt. As we have seen, Horney's three interpersonal movements or trends closely parallel many of Niebuhr's own descriptions of the dynamics of pride and sensuality. His primary objection to Horney is the same as his objection to

Erich Fromm, namely, her belief that the right social conditions may eventually free us from the self's dilemmas. Both Horney and Fromm offer brilliant insights and correct Freud's overemphasis on the death instinct. Yet they each make the opposite error of assuming that humanity can eventually heal itself of its estrangement problem. For Niebuhr, this form of utopianism is simply unrealistic because it denies the ongoing, human problem of existential anxiety. Because we are ontologically anxious, and not simply interpersonally anxious, we will always be tempted to act in destructive ways as we seek a form of security which is humanly impossible.

Because Niebuhr's primary focus has been on the dynamics of excessive self-regard and psychoanalysis has had a lot to say about narcissism, it may seem odd that Heinz Kohut, probably the foremost theorist on narcissism in psychoanalytic history, has been left out of the discussion. The reason is simple: I believe that Kohut's work is important enough that a full chapter contrasting Niebuhr and Kohut is warranted. It is to this comparison that I now turn.

4

Pride and Narcissism:
Niebuhr and Kohut on the Self

If the narcissistic self is so beset by shame, we need to resist moralistic condemnations and view narcissism more sympathetically. In this regard, the theological community has not been very helpful. . . .   —Donald Capps

When the self first begins to think of itself it thinks of itself first.
—Henri Bergson

In a previous publication, I explored the controversy concerning whether self-exaltation or self-devaluation is the more primary problem in the human condition.[1] I contrasted the Augustinian and Niebuhrian pride model with a humanistic low self-esteem model. I concluded with the belief, influenced heavily by Karen Horney, that pride and self-contempt are often two sides of the same coin. Beneath an outward display of arrogance hides a trembling insecurity; yet beneath an outward display of self-condemnation, a "pride system" often lurks, one which usually has completely unrealistic and inflated self-expectations. Thus, pride and low self-esteem often accompany each other in ways which may not appear obvious.

It is not my intension to repeat that argument here, but instead, to examine a pivotal figure who was left out of that discussion, Heinz Kohut. Many consider Kohut to be the most innovative and important psychoanalyst since Freud himself. As Charles Strozier puts it, "It is difficult to imagine a more original thinker in psychoanalysis after Freud than Heinz Kohut."[2] This originality, however, came only after a period of deep immersion in Freud's writings. It was not accidental that for many years Kohut was called "Mr.

---

[1]Terry D. Cooper, *Sin, Pride, and Self-Acceptance* (Downers Grove IL: InterVarsity Press, 2003).

[2]Charles Strozier, *Heinz Kohut: The Making of a Psychoanalyst* (New York: Other Press, 2001) xviii.

Psychoanalysis." As Strozier suggests, some may have known Freud's ideas as well, but no one knew them better than Kohut.[3]

Kohut worked hard to understand the relationship between a fragile, insecure self and narcissistic grandiosity. After focusing on the particular treatment of narcissistic personality disorders, Kohut gradually moved to the conviction that everyone struggles with the issue of narcissism and self-injury. While the disorder is more severe in some individuals, Kohut believed that the fragmented, injured self beneath narcissism is a universal concern. Thus, his theory about the treatment of a specific disorder (narcissism) was expanded into a more general theory of human development. Because Kohut is considered the primary psychological theorist on narcissism and Niebuhr is considered the primary theologian on the topic of excessive self-regard, a comparison of their thought is long overdue.

Kohut's Transformation of Freudian Narcissism

When Kohut came onto the psychoanalytic scene, narcissism had a very bad reputation. Freud essentially gave up on the possibility of treating narcissism. Freud believed that in healthy development, a child moves from (a) autoeroticism or a love of his or her isolated body parts, to (b) what he called *primary* narcissism or a love for oneself, to (c) object-love or love of others. These three shifts are crucial if the child is eventually able to love others. All the infant's original libidinal energy is directed at him or herself. Early frustrations interrupt these fantasies of omnipotence and grandeur. As infants are unable to achieve gratification through this primary narcissism, they turn their libidinal energy toward outside objects. Narcissitic libido thus turns into object libido in which their parents are their first love object. If this does not happen, then the child will be unable to connect with persons outside of him/herself. Sometimes disappointments in our attempts to love others can push us back toward self-love. This reinvestment of the libido back in oneself is called *secondary* narcissism. This involves a psychological withdrawal from the world. This secondary narcissism is most problematic because the person is not able to transfer feelings from previous relationships onto the analyst, have them brought to consciousness, and analyzed. Why? Because the narcissist, according to Freud, has not developed the necessary relationships with others which would allow such

---

[3]Strozier, *Heinz Kohut*, xxii.

a transference. A narcissist relates only to him or herself. There is nothing *to* transfer. The analyst must push the self-absorbed person to be more outwardly directed. If analysis is even possible at all, the analyst must expose and challenge narcissistic resistance, a process which will involve persistent and repetitive confrontation of the narcissist's use of arrogance and entitlement claims. Yet for the most part, because the narcissist is unable to transfer feelings from other relationships, analysis is as impossible as it is with a schizophrenic.

Note the crucial factor here in Freud's thought about narcissistic disorder: Self-love and object love are at war with each other. We must move *from* self-love *to* object love. Self-love will inevitably get in the way of healthy relationships. We only have a certain amount of libidinous energy to go around, and when we spend it on ourselves, we have nothing left for others. Another way of putting this is that Freud believed there is only *one line of development* from self-love to object love. Therefore, one cancels out the other.

Kohut eventually came to believe that this classical approach in treating narcissism is defective. It sees the narcissist as essentially "spoiled." The narcissist's grandiosity must have been greatly indulged and therefore needs to be punctured. The narcissistic defenses must be named, challenged, exposed, and interpreted. But Kohut believed that the deeper experience of the narcissist involves far more vulnerability than grandiosity. There is a sense in which, strange is it may sound, the classical Freudian model did not look "deeply" enough when dealing with narcissism. Beneath the obvious display of grandiosity is an injured self who has been deprived of the very attention he or she now so inappropriately seeks.

As we shall see, Kohut argued that self-love or narcissism and object-love have their own separate lines of development. Narcissism is thus not a lower form of object love or a primitive retreat from object-love. Instead, once again, it has its own history of development. It is therefore possible for self-love and object-love to coexist. The healthy end toward which narcissism nudges us is the development of ambitions, goals and achievements. Grandiosity therefore can be transformed into creativity. In fact, without this initial grandiosity, our productivity would suffer greatly. Both object-love and self-love undergo separate maturing processes.

Trauma or narcissistic injury disrupts the natural transformation of early grandiosity into healthy ambitions. In other words, the transition from grandiosity to energetic goals is stopped in its tracks. This more primitive grandiosity goes underground but it does not go away.

In a healthy climate, the child's parents offer empathy or emotional attentiveness, availability, and a kind of mirroring applause for the child's need for exhibitionism. This "adoring audience" is an important part of every child's development. When this kind of affirming attention is not available, the child's emerging sense of self is not "fed back" to him or her. In such a situation of narcissistic injury, the child may become fixated in this developmental need for attention. Adult attention seeking and audience craving usually represents a previous failure to get these needs met. At an *appropriate* time, the child's grandiosity was not recognized; now, at an *inappropriate* time in adulthood, the craving persists and makes strong demands on others. This mirror hunger persists in adult relationships. David Augsburger describes this process:

> If the person experiences the subject in the surrounding world as unavailable, nonempathic, and withholding understanding, the hungry self develops voracious narcissistic needs. When the rejection is extreme, the compensation for it by the empty self is also extreme. The unfulfilled needs leave gaps in the formation of the self, missing pieces in the self-structure.[4]

Unmet narcissistic needs from childhood, therefore, can create problems for adult relationships, particularly when we expect the other to serve as an adoring audience. While parents can never perfectly provide this empathic environment for the child—nor do they need to—they can offer a supportive and attentive environment. Traumatic failures or shame can lead to severe disturbances in the transformation of narcissism into healthy self-regard. But Kohut recognized that all parents, no matter how committed, inevitably fail sometimes. He frequently called this "optimal frustration" because it helps the child eventually move toward more self-reliance. Many psychoanalytic self psychologists now prefer to call it optimal responsiveness.[5]

When parents are performing this crucial task for the child, Kohut refers to them as "self-objects/selfobjects."[6] By that, he simply means that the

---

[4]David Augsburger, *Helping People Forgive* (Louisville: Westminster/John Knox Press, 1996) 75.

[5]See *Advances in Self-Psychology*, ed. Arnold Goldberg (New York: International Universities Press, 1980).

[6]In his early writings Kohut coined "self-object"; later he removed the

parents are considered part of the child's resources for dealing with life. The parent offers the child certain *functions* which the child interprets as part of his/her own arsenal of skills. Eventually, the child will internalize those functions and be able to perform them without parental intervention. Having watched a parent soothe the child, the child eventually learns some things about self-soothing when the parent is not around. The child has learned to imitate this skill for him/herself and can engage in self-calming. Throughout his writings, Kohut refers to this phenomenon as "transmuting internalizations." Perhaps a simple illustration will help. Suppose I am dependent on someone else to cook my breakfast each morning. This is a skill that I simply don't have and so it creates a need for a selfobject to offer this service. However, as I watch the process of cooking, I begin to internalize it and become able to cook breakfast for myself, which may indeed be a relief to the other person. And what if the task or function the other person performs is psychological, rather than breakfast preparation? The same would apply. For instance, I might at first desperately need someone to help me "calm down" when I get angry. I may even expect or demand that they immediately respond. However, after having watched the way they psychologically function with me, I may be able to engage in some self-soothing. I can do for myself what someone else had to do for me. When I incorporate these functions supplied by selfobjects, I create a more solid sense of self. And further, I am then able to offer myself as a selfobject for another. As psychoanalyst Volney Gay puts it, "If all goes well, children whose parents have served such selfobject roles will themselves become capable of soothing others. Hence, there is a natural progress from the child's state of requiring a great deal of selfobject relatedness from the child's environment, to performing these functions for the child's self, to becoming a selfobject for others."[7]

Another important need of the child is to idealize the parent. By idealizing a parent, the child is able to look up to a parent and feel strong by virtue of a connection to this strong "other." It is vicarious strength. Alone, the child does not feel strong, but by virtue of his or her connection to the parent—who *is* strong—the child can also feel solid. The child, then, needs to feel part of something larger than him/herself. Put another way, the child

hyphen—"selfobject."

[7]Volnery P. Gay, *Understanding the Occult: Fragmentation and Repair of the Self* (Minneapolis: Fortress Press, 1989) 28.

needs to "borrow" the parents' strength in order to eventually develop his or her own robust sense of self. This parental infallibility will eventually be demystified, but for a period in the child's early life, it is crucial.

So for Kohut, it is perfectly legitimate for the young child to be exhibitionistic in a display of grandiosity. When properly mirrored and empathically understood, this grandiosity will be transformed into energetic ambitions and enthusiasm. The need for an adoring audience will fade and the need to excel and fulfill one's potential will replace it. Similarly, the idealization of one's parents will turn into a more modest source of guidance and values for one's life. The common assumption might be that too much attention turns a child into a narcissist; in reality, Kohut is saying the opposite. The adult hunger for attention is severe because attention was not given at the age-appropriate time. As Augsburger puts it,

> narcissism—the self overconcerned with itself—is the self's attempt to substitute self-indulgent self-care for the appropriate care by a significant other which is absent or woefully inadequate. The self-centered behavior of the narcissist arises from too little self-esteem and self-valuation, not from too much. It is the impoverished self that hungrily grasps for attention and affirmation (no matter how smoothly presented or artfully expressed).[8]

So once again, when this process of mirroring and idealization fail, the older narcissist tries desperately to substitute excessive attention, flattery, or power for what has been developmentally missing. While the narcissist may occasionally find someone who is willing to serve as an adoring audience, most individuals will run out of patience fairly quickly. It is even difficult for therapists who work with narcissistic patients. The reason is that the narcissist is so dismissive of another person, often not even "seeing" the other person in the room. The only purpose of another person is to serve as a mirror holder so that the narcissist can see him/herself reflected back. Adult narcissists seek *narcissistic supplies* and not relationships. Others are instruments of attention, an audience whose only function is to watch the performance. The narcissist is completely dependent on others for this attention because he or she has not internalized the ability to self-sooth. Without reassuring, soothing parents, the child has never learned to reassure him/herself.

---

[8]Augsburger, *Helping People Forgive*, 76.

The Source of Pathology

For Kohut, psychopathology always results from insufficient self-cohesion. Self-fragmentation and psychological sickness go hand in hand. Kohut says, "it is the specific pathogenic personality of the parent(s) and specifically pathogenic features of the atmosphere in which the child grows up that account for the maldevelopments, fixations, and unsolvable inner conflicts characterizing the adult personality."[9] Crayton Rowe and David MacIssac further describe the significance of parental attentiveness and empathy for self-psychology:

> [F]or the self-psychologists, the origin of psychopathology is not so much a specific traumatic event or even a specific child-rearing philosophy. The major issue here is whether or not the parents have adequate self-structure in their own development. It is the parents' security and self-confidence that allows them to meet their children's selfobject needs without resentment, and/or without the need to compete in some way with their children to satisfy their own unfulfilled needs.[10]

Narcissistic parents deprive their children of narcissistic satisfaction because they are preoccupied with their own needs. Self-injury thus gets passed on from one generation to another.[11] The child is unable to adequately develop a self-structure because this sense of self is not adequately mirrored. As Strozier puts it, "the child remains fixated on the primitive images of the other, and will be forever dependent on substitute figures in what can only be described as an 'intense form of object hunger.' The hunger is intense because such people are looking for 'missing segments' in their psychic structure."[12] Others are desperately needed to fulfill what is lacking in self-structure. Stated more simply, others are always necessary to do for us what we cannot do for ourselves.

---

[9]Heinz Kohut, *The Restoration of the Self* (New York: International Universities Press, 1977) 187.

[10]Crayton E. Rowe, Jr. and David S. MacIaac, *Empathic Attunement: the Technique of Psychoanalytic Self Psychology* (Northvale NJ: Jacob Aronson, 1989) 78.

[11]See Alice Miller, *The Drama of the Gifted Child*, trans. Ruth Ward (New York: Basic Books, 1981).

[12]Srozier, *Heinz Kohut*, 199.

The Importance of Empathy

Kohut once stated, "The best definition of empathy . . . is that it is the capacity to think and feel oneself into the inner life of another person."[13] For Kohut, empathy is the only means of truly understanding the psychological world of another human being. It is a means of gathering psychological data, and not simply a warm and fuzzy experience. It is vicarious introspection. As Rowe and MacIssac put it, "Self psychology believes that the empathic experience-near mode of gathering data can bring about the deepest level of understanding complex mental states. The empathic process is employed solely as a scientific tool to enable the analyst to eventually make interpretations to the patient that are as accurate and as complete as possible."[14] Kohut gradually began to realize that he was far more than a blank screen on which his patients could transfer their displaced anger and sexual conflicts. Instead, by offering his patients empathy, he was providing a psychological service or function which the patient had not previously experienced. He was allowing himself to be used as a selfobject because this is precisely what the fragmented patient needed. This empathic participation in the patient's experience gradually supplied the very thing which was missing in patient's childhood, namely, mirroring and idealization. The patient needs to feel profoundly understood in a nonjudgmental way. Put another way, the analyst must allow the grandiosity to come forth without challenging or confronting it. Because the grandiosity emerges from a developmental deficiency, the analyst should not prematurely interpret it.

Kohut and Kernberg: Empathy vs. Confrontation

Kohut differs significantly from another major psychoanalytic theorist of narcissism, Otto Kernberg. Kernberg argues that adult narcissistic pathology and childhood narcissism are quite different.[15] For Kernberg, the grandiosity of adult narcissism needs to be rigorously challenged and interpreted. Kohut, on the other hand, attends to the sense of deficiency underlying the grandiosity. As a general rule, those theorists who emphasize grandiosity

---

[13]Heinz Kohut, *How Does Analysis Cure?* (Chicago: University of Chicago Press, 1984) 82.

[14]Rowe and MacIssac, *Empathic Attunement*, 64.

[15]Otto Kernberg, *Borderline Conditions and Pathological Narcissism* (New York: Jason Aronson, 1975) 270-342.

as the primary problem are more confrontational, whereas those who emphasize deficiency are more supportive. While analysts recognize that both grandiosity and self-deficiency coexist, the question is which one takes priority. The subjective experience of the narcissist often moves from the low end of shame, envy, emptiness, incompleteness, ugliness and inferiority to the high end of compensatory feelings such as self-righteousness, pride, contempt for others, defensive self-sufficiency, vanity, and superiority. For Kohut, as we have seen, the fragile, deficient self which is "behind" the grandiosity needs to be supported. And empathy is the key.

For Kernberg, on the other hand, narcissism is *not* a fixation at a normal state of development. It is instead a pathological defense which results from the conflict generated by unconscious rage against persons who have humiliated us or abandoned us as children. The influence of Melanie Klein on Kernberg is clear.[16] The narcissist has enormous rage. The adult's "grandiose self," then, is quite different for Kernberg than the child's early narcissism.[17] Childhood self-centeredness is warm and engaging. Children "show off" for someone they love. Adult narcissists, on the other hand, may be superficially charming but they are invested in no one. They are only interested in narcissistic supplies. Childhood narcissism can also be gratified. Children can enjoy the attention. Adult narcissism, on the other hand, has an insatiable quality to it. Adult narcissists are never satisfied. There is also an element of far greater aggression in adult narcissism. The adult narcissist is enormously envious and seeks to destroy the other simply because he or she appears better than oneself. Further, small children's need for attention has a more realistic quality than the need of the grandiose adult narcissist. And children's narcissism coexists with both a love for mom and dad and a trust and dependence that their parents are reliable sources for attention. Adult narcissists, argues Kernberg, don't love or trust others except for temporary shots of attention.

Stated simply, Kernberg's theory of narcissism is much more harsh than Kohut's. Yet for Kernberg, it is much more realistic. Again, Kernberg does *not* believe that narcissistic personality disorder results soley from nar-

---

[16]Melanie Klein argued that destructive aggression is biologically driven. See *Love, Guilt, and Reparation, and Other Works, 1921–1945*, vol. 1 of *The Writings of Melanie Klein*, ed. with an intro. by Roger Money-Kyrle (New York: The Free Press, 1975).

[17]Kernberg, *Borderline Conditions and Pathological Narcissim*, 272-73.

cissistic frustration or attention deprivation in childhood. In fact, for Kernberg, Kohut does not do justice to the issues of destructive rage, envy, and resentment in narcissism. Kernberg believes, along with Klein, that we have a built-in destructive capacity for rage which can be used in the service of devaluing another. We want to destroy the very source we need in order to eliminate our own envy. The adult grandiose self feels powerless and therefore wants to destroy what others offer because she hates her own helplessness. Envy and rage underlie grandiosity. Thus Kernberg looks for the tendency to devalue others—including the analyst—when working with narcissistic patients.

Kohut, on the other hand, would ask Kernberg why the patient *wants* to devalue others. Is it not because they, themselves, have been devalued? When one feels unloved and unredeemable, it is natural to want to bring down the rest of the world to one's level. There are enormous feelings of abandonment, loneliness, and yearning beneath this destructive envy. Kohut would no doubt say that a major part of his difference with Kernberg is directly related to their opposing views on destructive aggression. Once again, for Kernberg, innate, destructive, aggressive drives are always a part of the picture. These innate drives may be triggered by frustration, but they are already present and ready to lunge forth. For Kohut, on the other hand, destructive aggression is a frustration reaction and by-product of narcissistic deprivation. In other words, Kernberg remains loyal to classic Freudian drive theory whereas Kohut does not. Stephen Mitchell and Margaret Black state Kohut's position well:

> How does the child emerge from these childhood narcissistic states? Not, Kohut came to believe, by confronting their unrealistic features. The child who is swooping around the living room in his Superman cape needs to have his exuberance enjoyed, not have his fantasies interpreted as grandiose. The child who believes that his mother makes the sun rise in the morning needs to be allowed to enjoy his participation in the divine, not to be informed of his mother's diminutive status in the universe. These early narcissistic states of mind contain the kernels of healthy narcissism; they must be allowed slow transformation on their own, Kohut suggested, simply by virtue of exposure to reality. The child comes to appreciate the unrealistic nature of his views himself and his parents as he suffers the ordinary disappointments and disillusions of everyday life: he can't walk through walls, her father cannot decree that her soccer team will always win, and so on. In healthy development, the inflated images of self and other are whittled down, little by little, to more or less realistic proportions. Inevitable yet manageable, optimal

frustration will take place within a generally supportive environment. Against this secure backdrop, the child rises to the occasion, survives the frustration or disappointment, and in the process internalizes functional features of the selfobject.[18]

Rather than quickly interpreting the patient's grandiosity as Kernberg might do, Kohut feels that an empathic reflection of this grandiosity is necessary in order for the person to move beyond it. The mirroring, nurturing experience addresses the narcissistic injuries that keep these patients from moving forward. If the analyst is persistent in this empathy, followed by a more gentle interpretation of what is interpretation of what the patient is experiencing, a healthy development will emerge. Again, however, the emphasis must be upon the injurious impact of the child's early psychological environment rather than on the primitive urges arising from within. This will require a great deal of time and patience from the analyst.

It is important to note here, however, that for Kohut, empathy alone is not enough. The other great twentieth-century theorist of empathy, Carl Rogers, enormously highlighted the significance of empathic understanding, but essentially argued that empathy, alone, is curative. Rogers trusted the client to come to his her own interpretation of experience once the foundation of empathy, unconditional positive regard, and congruence had been laid.[19] For Kohut, empathy also needs interpretation. While all effective interpretation is clearly an *outgrowth* of empathy, the empathy alone is not satisfactory. Effective analysis must involve both empathy and explanation. While Rogers offered empathy without explanation and many traditional psychoanalysts offered explanation without empathy, Kohut attempted to offer *both*. While some patients may need a very long period of empathy, an explanation of the patient's psychodynamics will also be necessary.

Drives and Innate Destructiveness

Earlier, we saw that Niebuhr rejected any notion that our fundamental nature or being is destructive or essentially sinful. Put another way, our sin

---

[18]Stephen A. Mitchell and Margaret J. Black, *Freud and Beyond* (New York: Basic Books, 1995) 159-60.

[19]Carl Rogers, "The Interpersonal Relationship: The Core of Guidance," in Rogers et al., *Person to Person: The Problem of Being Human* (New York: Pocket Books, 1971) 85-101.

does not emerge from beastly drives we need to beat down and tame. For this reason, Niebuhr argued against Freud's biological reduction of humanity's ills. Similarly, Kohut parts company with Freud's drive theory. As Kohut states it:

> The baby cries, and the baby cries angrily when whatever needs to be done is not done immediately. But there is no original need to destroy; the original need is to establish an equilibrium. . . . Speaking in biological terms, we will, of course, acknowledge the presence of a preformed apparatus (teeth and nails and muscles) that determines the specific patterns in which the continuum assertiveness-aggression-destructiveness manifest itself. But, psychoanalytically speaking, the human baby is not comparable to a beast of prey.[20]

Destructive aggression does not emerge naturally in the same way that hunger or other bodily needs do. Instead, it is the result of frustration. It is largely for this reason that Kohut had little use for Melanie Klein, even though he was quite familiar with her work. As Strozier reminds us, Kohut thought there was something rather perverse about the way Klein understood and described the baby as evil.[21] For instance, Klein believed the nursing infant had violent fantasies about his or her mother's breast.[22] She considered herself the "true daughter of Sigmund Freud" because she maintained a rigorous belief in the death instinct. Kohut responds to the notion of innate destructiveness in the human infant in a similar way that Niebuhr responds to the idea that sin is transmitted biologically. In both cases, the criticism was against any idea that our primary problem is rooted in biology.

Classical psychoanalysis and drive theory are practically synonymous. The source of motivation, from this perspective, is located in the biological sphere. Most of the early splits from Freudian psychoanalysis concerned conflicts over the issue of drive theory. For Freud, the ego and Superego must rechannel or sublimate the biological drives into socially acceptable behavior. Instinctual impulses seek expression but run into the rules neces-

---

[20]Heinz Kohut, *The Chicago Institute Lectures*, ed. by Paul Tolpin and Marian Tolpin (Hillsdale NJ: Analytic Press, 1996) 199-201.

[21]Strozier, *Heinz Kohut*, 225.

[22]For an excellent review of Klein's theory of the infant's hatred, see Christopher Monte, *Beneath the Mask*, 6th ed. (Fort Worth TX: Harcourt Brace, 1999) esp. 263-65.

sary for civilization to survive. Put simply, instincts bump into prohibitions. As we saw in chapter 3, Freud believed early in his career that the primary goal of psychoanalysis was to eliminate the repression which keeps these drives bottled up. Yet as he grew older, he came to believe that a direct expression of these biological drives would render civilization impossible.

Kohut, on the other hand, made a huge break with Freudian theory when he argued that destructive sexual and aggressive impulses are not primary drives, but instead, secondary products. Kohut puts it this way:

> When we analyze adults who suffer from narcissistic disturbances—individuals who make incessant demands for gratification, we may get the impression that they were spoiled as children. We reason: there was continuous drive gratification, so those people became fixated on their drives and that is why they became sick. But that's not so. They didn't become fixated on the drive because they were spoiled, because of drive gratification. They became fixated on drives because they their budding selves were overlooked, were not responded to. They turned to drive gratification (and later remained fixed on it) because they tried to relieve their depression—they tried to escape the horrible feeling that nobody was responding to them. Such people may have had mothers who satisfied their drives continuously, yet failed to respond with pride and pleasure to the child's independent self.[23]

Note what Kohut is saying here, namely, that drive preoccupations are an outgrowth of narcissistic injury. They are a substitute for the deeper need to be affirmed, attended to, and recognized for who we are. It is because the *entire self* is not empathically mirrored that fixations on particular drives emerge. Thus, the drives are a by-product of narcissistic injury. So-called "spoiled brat" kids may appear the way they do *not* so much because they have been given "too much," but because they have not been given the right things. Clearly, many parents shower their children with material possessions the whole time that they are psychologically abandoning them.

But if the drives are secondary products, then what is the primary problem? Kohut's answer: self-injury. In other words, our problems with sexual and aggressive tendencies are actually disintegrative by-products of an injured self. They represent self-deficits and not primary biological expressions of an unruly id. Kohut is *not* denying the existence of destructive impulses. Nor is he saying that destructiveness is not real and

---

[23]Kohut, *The Chicago Institute Lectures*, 208-209.

attempting to see the world through rose-colored glasses. But he *is* asking about the source of these impulses. Rather than seeing them as direct biological expressions, he sees them instead as secondary reactions to a deeper problem, namely, the empathic failures which had led to self-rupture. The outcome of this belief involves seeing the pre-Oedipal issues in a child's life as more significant than the traditional psychoanalytic pre-occupation with Oedipal issues. In other words, the sexual and aggressive issues connected with the Oedipal conflict actually *reveal a process of self-disintegration which has already taken place.* The so-called Oedipus complex is a major problem only when the self has already been injured. It does not *have* to be the source of neurosis as traditional psychoanalysis has believed.

Rejecting the central significance of the Oedipal complex is one of the easiest ways to get booted out of the club of traditional psychoanalysis. The Oedipus complex has been seen as the bedrock of neurosis, the primary breeding ground for adult problems. Yet Kohut declares that the intensity of the Oedipal issue is problematic because of earlier experience.

Also, classical psychoanalysis argued that the ego and superego must defend against the hidden wishes and instincts of the id. The analyst must be an objective scientist who gets behind these defenses and interprets them. Kohut, on the other hand, saw resistance as a patient's reluctance to be in a narcissistically vulnerable situation. Defensiveness can, in fact, emerge as an attempt to maintain the cohesiveness of the self. Defenses are not so much things which must be torn down or pushed aside. Instead, the analyst needs to look at how resistance had been an adaptive strategy. As Rowe and MacIssac put it, "for Kohut, resistance is an expression of creative psychological adaptation that has allowed the individual to cope with less than optimal early environmental circumstances."[24] Also, Kohut believed that in many instances the patient becomes resistant *because of* the analyst's empathic failures. Kohut therefore accepts some of the responsibility for a patient's defensiveness. It is perhaps due to his own lack of understanding.

Thus, Kohut's position is crucial to grasp: Competitiveness and healthy aggression are natural, but destructive aggression is not. Destructive rage is a breakdown product of the deeper issue of narcissistic injury. Destructive anger results not from our bodies but from our nonempathic environments. Healthy aggression is time limited and lasts only while we

---

[24]Rowe and MacIssac, *Empathic Attunement*, 99.

are pursuing a goal; destructive aggression, on the other hand, is nonproductive and results from an injured self. As Volney Gay puts it, "From a moralistic point of view, the patient's rage is wrong and unjustified. From an empathic, analytic point of view these rageful responses, like fragmentation experiences, must be understood as signs of the patient's profound narcissistic suffering."[25] When the analyst is experienced by the patient as uninvested or unempathic, a great deal of rage may come forth. Many analysts will understand this rage as nothing more than unrealistic entitlement claims which need to be challenged. But Kohut began to notice that this rage was related to perceived lapses of empathy. The analyst's lack of understanding seemed to trigger a deep narcissistic wound. The rage may seem overreactionary because it signals a self-fracture which is unhealed. Empathic failure creates fragmentation anxiety which then shields itself with rage. But the analyst must see past this rage and be attuned to the self-fragmentation and hurt which are beneath it.

Again, the rage, for Kohut, is not based on innate drives but upon deep narcissistic wounds. Gaps in empathy bring on the patient's feeling of falling apart. Self-esteem is deregulated and the patient frequently reacts to the experience with hostility. But the Kohutian analyst works empathically *through* this hostile reaction. The patient's anger, too, needs to be understood empathically. And then eventually, the empathic analyst can help the patient realize how this rage is linked to feelings of narcissistic injury. But the empathic understanding *must come first*. Interpretation must be an outgrowth of empathy. Questions about the appropriateness of these rageful outbursts must be bracketed. Thus Kohut's message is clear: We need to quit *moralizing* the condition of narcissism. It's easy to be revolted by someone's obvious grandiosity. It's ugly. But if we want to help heal them, we will need to see beneath it. And this may mean allowing ourselves to be a "punching bag" for a while. Eventually, as the rage runs out of steam and the empathic understanding helps the person feel more cohesive and less fragmentary, the analyst can help with interpretation. If, on the other hand, one believes, as does Kernberg, that the narcissitic rage comes from a biological drive itself, then such empathic immersion is not necessary. Yet for Kohut, narcissists who do not receive empathy will not be cured. This is essentially the point in his famous case study, "The Two Analyses of Mr.

---

[25]Volney P. Gay, *Understanding the Occult: Fragmentation and Repair of the Self* (Minneapolis: Fortress Press, 1989) 41.

Z."[26] In the first analysis of Mr. Z, Kohut was still working from the standpoint of drive theory in a manner similar to Kernberg. In the second analysis, however, Kohut recognized the radical importance of empathy in dealing with the nonbiological rage which accompanies narcissistic injury. The rage, then, is never the *primary* problem.

As Strozier puts it, "The most gruesome destructiveness, Kohut says, is not the result of wildly regressive and primitive behavior; it is 'orderly and organized activities' in which the perpetrators' destructiveness is alloyed with absolute conviction about their greatness and with their devotion to archaic omnipotent figures."[27] This comment sounds almost identical to a Niebuhrian conception of pride.

What is perhaps most crucial to recognize in Kohut's developing thought is his conviction that the same injured self which lies behind narcissistic personality disorders is also the source of all other psychological disorders. The injured, wounded or fragmented self, then, became the focus of his entire therapeutic method. Psychoanalysis has really been trying to heal internal splits or divisions within the self. The point is pulling together various fragments of the self. Whereas Freud had fluctuated back and forth between the words "ego" and "self," Kohut was now making the self the primary factor in his new psychoanalytic self psychology. For him, the self is "a unit, cohesive in space and enduring in time, which is a center of initiative and a recipient of impressions."[28] Pathology, then, results from insufficient self-cohesion. The process of analysis is therefore devoted to help strengthen and build up the sense of self. This psychic structure will then provide resources for regulating self-esteem. Much of disturbed behavior has in fact been an attempt to compensate for a lack of internal self structure.

Self-Injury and Addiction

For Kohut, as we have seen, when children lack healthy selfobjects who can reflect back to them who they are, they are unable to internalize those soothing functions provided by the selfobjects. This failure at incorporating

---

[26]Heinz Kohut, "The Two Analyses of Mr. Z," *International Journal of Psychoanalysis* 60 (1979): 3-27.

[27]Strozier, *Heinz Kohut*, 250.

[28]Heinz Kohut, *The Analysis of the Self* (New York: International Universities Press, 1971) vii.

the functions of healthy selfobjects leads to difficulty regulating self-esteem, as well as a general inability to provide any degree of self-comfort. Others are ongoingly necessary to provide a function which one is impaired from providing oneself. In a similar way, alcohol, other drugs, or addictive behavior can be employed in an attempt to provide this much needed function. As Jerome Levin puts it, "Alcohol, through its pharmacological properties, readily performs the normal functions of affect regulation, stimulus attenuation, and self-soothing by anesthetizing painful or uncomfortable drives, emotions, and sensations."[29] Kohut describes, rather brilliantly, addiction as an attempt to find a nurturing partner:

> The addict . . . craves the drug because the drug seems to him capable of curing the central defect in his self. It becomes for him the substitute for a self-object which failed him traumatically at the time when he should still have had the feeling of omnipotently controlling its responses in accordance with his needs as if it were part of himself. By ingesting the drug he symbolically compels the mirroring self-object to soothe him, to accept him. Or he symbolically compels the idealized self-object to submit to his merging into it and thus to his partaking of its magical power. In any case the ingestion of the drug provides him with the self-esteem which he does not possess. Through the incorporation of the drug he supplies for himself the feeling of being accepted and thus of being self-confident; he craves the experience of being merged with a source of power that gives him the feeling of being stronger and worthwhile. And all these effects of the drug tend to increase his feeling of being alive, tend to increase his certainty that he exists in the world. . . . It is the tragedy of . . . these attempts at self-cure that . . . they cannot succeed . . . no psychic structure is built, the defect in the self remains.[30]

As long as we do not minimize the biological component of addiction, this Kohutian insight into substances or addictive activities (gambling, shopping, sex, and so on) as much-needed self-objects is quite revealing. Every chemical dependency counselor knows that the addict has a *relationship* with the chemical. Even while the drug is destructive, the addict comes to believe that the drug provides the function of self-esteem regulation and self solidification. While the addict's life may be falling apart, the drug seems to hold the addict together. This is why chemically dependent indi-

---

[29]Jerome D. Levin, *Treatment of Alcoholism and Other Addictions: A Self-Psychology Approach* (Northvale NJ: Jason Aronson, 1987) 238.

[30]Quoted in Levin, *Treatment of Alcoholism and Other Addictions*, 325-26.

viduals often think they cannot survive without the drug. While those around them recognize that the drug is killing them, for the addict, giving up the drug would amount to their psychological "undoing." Again, to quote Kohut:

> It is the structural void in the self that the addict tries to fill—whether by sexual activity or by oral ingestion. And the structural void cannot be filled any better by oral ingestion than by any other addictive behavior. It is the lack of self-esteem of the unmirrored self, the uncertainty about the very existence of the self, the dreadful feeling of the fragmentation of the self that the addict tries counteract by his addictive behavior.[31]

Unfortunately, even though the addict may think the drug regulates his or her self-esteem, it actually does not. In fact, it heightens the polarities between grandiosity and shame. In an intoxicated state, the self may feel invincible, on top of the world, or utterly full of itself. Yet as the drug wears off, shame frequently overwhelms the psyche, driving the person back to another drink or drug. The movement is from arrogance to self-loathing but it never involves a solid sense of self. Self-confidence is lacking. A common expression in recovery groups is, "I'm an egomaniac with an inferiority complex." There is more wisdom in this comment than might first appear. Reliance on the drug as an ego-boosting self-object actually deteriorates the self's own structure and ability to function. The result is a roller coaster which goes from inflated grandiosity to deflated shame and humiliation.

For Kohut, then, the psychological dynamics of addiction are driven by a sense of self-fracture. Unruly desires are related to a disturbance in the self. This position is not dissimilar from the Augustinian and Niebuhrian view that concupiscence, or excessive desire, is an outgrowth of self-preoccupation. As we have seen in earlier chapters, Niebuhr followed Augustine's conviction that so-called "excessive desires" are not the primary problem. There is a rupture in our relationship with God, our neighbors, and ourselves which precedes the process of addictive attachment. We become fixated on the pleasures of the flesh because something is fundamentally wrong with our primary relationships. The anxieties of life promote a temptation to distrust God and make ourselves the center of our own lives. Trying to overcome this inevitable and ineradicable anxiety, we

---

[31]Kohut, *The Restoration of the Self*, 197.

obsess on ourselves or drown ourselves in sensuality. Whether its self-exaltation or self-avoidance, the genuine self is lost in the process. True self-confidence is lost because of our need to bolster a grandiose and godlike self which can handle anything. We do not want to have to depend on anything; we are the center of life. We may feel overwhelmed that we escape the burdens and ambiguities of selfhood by worshipping someone else and orbiting our lives completely around them. We may insist that everyone treat us like a god. Or we may simply escape the pains of self-consciousness through some form of intoxicating escape, whether it takes the form of chemicals or activities. The point is that the essential self is lost in each of these processes. In fact, it tries to "correct" the problem by either exalting its own powers or excessively relying on untrustworthy selfobjects. Because our anxiety concerns ultimate or infinite matters, all finite selfobjects will prove unsuccessful.

Kohut and Postmodernism

Sometimes conceptual changes happen very fast. A mere thirty years ago, Kohut's ideas were thought to be utterly revolutionary. Now, thirty years later, some radical postmodern thinkers see Kohut as already out of date. They have criticized him for his so-called "modern" tendencies.[32] These modern tendencies have included the belief in an abiding, unitary sense of self; the attempt to put forth a universal narrative about the human condition; an effort to arrive at a consistent and enduring psychological theory; and a failure to realize that the self is completely constructed in each social encounter. Teicholz, however, views Kohut as having his theoretical feet in modernity *and* postmodernity.[33] This issue is complex and beyond the scope of this book's aims. But perhaps it is important to examine a few of the ways in which Kohut may not be as "guilty" of a modernist directive as some postmodernists claim. On the other hand, some of his modernist impulses may still be very valid and important. Being "modern," in itself, is certainly not a cognitive sin. In fact, one can make a fairly strong case that the perspectives of some radical postmodern thinkers is ultimately self-defeating. It is one thing to move away from the errors of foundationalism,

---

[32]For an excellent summary and critique of Kohut and postmodernism, see Judith Guss Teicholz, *Kohut, Loewald, and the Postmoderns: A Comparative Study of Self and Relationship* (Hillsdale NJ: Analytic Press, 1999).

[33]Teicholz, *Kohut, Loewald, and the Postmoderns*, 18-19.

or the belief that one can find an epistemologically innocent place to begin one's theorizing. Yet it is quite another to embrace an extreme form of relativism in which dialogue is reduced to simply sharing personal tastes. Saying that we cannot know the "Truth" with absolute certainty is a far cry from saying that all perspectives are equally close to it.

Kohut is sometimes charged with so emphasizing a solid, autonomous self that he failed to consider the relational or interpersonal aspect of so-called "self" formation. Yet Kohut believed that our sense of self comes into being largely as a result of *being treated* as a whole self. It is a completely relational process in which we will need selfobjects throughout our lives. As Kohut put it:

> Throughout his life a person will experience himself as a cohesive harmonious firm unit in time and space, connected with his past and pointing meaningfully into a creative-productive future, [but] only as long as, at each stage in his life, he experiences certain representations of his human surroundings as joyfully responding to him, as available to him as sources of idealized strength and calmness, as being silently present but in essence like him.[34]

It is important to accent the fact that Kohut believed the self needs selfobjects *throughout the lifespan*. While it is true that the early childhood needs for selfobjects may be more archaic and intense than later adult needs, it is nonetheless true that relationships nourish the self in adulthood as well. Selfobjects are necessary in childhood to help kids form a self structure; they are necessary in adulthood to enhance and maintain that structure. In adulthood, the relationships will be more reciprocal or mutual. In marriage, for instance, partners will offer each other support when the other's sense of self feels weak or fragile. But the roles go back and forth. When one partner is *always* the supplier of the other's selfobject needs, resentment festers and the relationship is in danger. In fact, it may be very difficult indeed to find someone who can offer narcissistic supplies to a deeply injured person. This is why we need analysts. The analyst provides this selfobject function without calculating the reciprocity in the relationship. But even in analysis, as we have seen, the goal is for the patient to eventually internalize the analyst's function and learn to self-sooth. And the goal is *not* to teach people how to self-sooth so that they will no longer need

---

[34]Heinz Kohut, *How Does Analysis Cure?* (Chicago: University of Chicago Press, 1984) 52.

relationships. They will *always* need relationships.

Also, by "self," Kohut did not mean a rigid, "fixed," unchanging structure. This sort of construct, in Kohut's mind, would have been experience-distant, rather than experience-near. For Kohut, this sense of "I-ness" is open to change, but it *does* have a sense of continuity and cohesion. As Teicholtz puts it, "I think that Kohut may have meant that we need a sense of continuity *because* of the complexity and multifaceted nature of our lives and our psyches, *because* of the multiplicity of our roles and relationships."[35] And perhaps the question becomes this: Can any thinker, regardless how radically postmodern he or she claims to be, really "get along" without a sense of self? Teicholz puts this issue sharply:

> Although Lacan, Barratt, and others seem to insist that we can and must give up this illusory sense of self, it is difficult for me to imagine that Barratt himself, for instance, without the sense of self or identity that he theoretically rejects as a foreclosure, could have decided on a project of value and interest to him, such as a book on the postmodern impulse, carried out the sustained research necessary to implement it, and motivated and organized himself to do the writing. In other words, without such concepts as ambitions, goals, and ideals in the Kohutian sense, now can we understand the processes through which any personally meaningful project is chosen, sustained, and implemented?[36]

The fact that the self is not a "thing" does not mean that it has no reality or meaning. A more cohesive, robust sense of self can be a goal of therapy without becoming a restraint and obstacle to a fuller experience of life.

"Theologizing" Kohut?

Perhaps it might be helpful if we apply Kohut's analysis to two of the most important stories in the shaping of Western thought. These are cosmic stories, first of Satan and then later of Adam and Eve in the Garden of Eden. In Kohut's cosmic drama, perhaps the primary problem of Satan—the ultimate symbol of evil—is that he emerged in destructive form after empathic failure. He did not primarily choose out of his freedom to replace God or surpass the Divine in power and significance. Instead, he found himself in the predicament of not being adequately mirrored. Satan's exhibi-

---

[35]Teicholz, *Kohut, Loewald, and the Postmoderns*, 53.
[36]Teicholz, *Kohut, Loewald, and the Postmoderns*, 55.

tionistic self was not adequately affirmed. He became stuck in a kind of primitive grandiosity. Wounded and insecure, he arrogantly camouflages a deep conviction that his not freely accepted as he is. His destructiveness and envy of God are part of his narcissistic rage. His aggression is a disintegration by-product, a cosmic acting out in which he wants to destroy everything and make it as miserable as he is. Theologically, he believes that he is now outside the parameters of Divine grace and is henceforth in perpetual rebellion. He is at war with his own desire for God, trying desperately to convince himself that he can stand alone without a need for Divine empathy and affirmation. His evil is a form of pride but it is a wounded pride which seeks to hide its underlying hopelessness. Put another way, the Devil is in despair.

With a bit of a theological stretch, one could use Origen—rather than Augustine—as a religious interpreter of this Kohutian rift between Satan and God. Even Satan, according to Origen, will eventually lay down his fruitlessly destructive path and accept the empathic love of God. All things will ultimately be restored. But again, this will occur from empathic love and *not* from a confrontational assault. Love, not wrath, will be the final healing agent.

Augustine, of course, had given up on Satan and believed that the distortion of his will is what has led to his permanent violation of God's will. There will be no final cosmic healing such as Origen envisioned. Thus, his semidualism ends up with an eternal universe in which everything is in its "proper" place. Satan, the demons, and the nonelect will be forever separated from God, the angels, and the elect. We saw earlier that Jung could never be satisfied with this ultimate dualism. Kohut would probably not be either.

A Kohutian interpretation of the story of Adam and Eve would have similar results. Adam and Eve may have been tempted to eat of the forbidden tree because they felt inadequate, insecure, and inferior to God. Feeling this sense of inadequacy, they tried to be more than human. A lack of self-affirmation propelled them into a desire to be like God.

Niebuhr, however, would argue that this mythical story makes a very important point, namely, that the Garden of Eden symbolizes the fact that the first couple had all the resources they needed for human flourishing. The Fall cannot be blamed on God's empathic failure. It is humanity's attempt to reach beyond itself, to deny its own finitude, and to crave a godlike status which fuels the Fall. Put another way, it's not primarily a problem of *deprivation*. The central factor is that humanity is not content with its finite status and instead craves a Divine status. Even with all the provisions necessary, sin still happens. As we have seen, this is Niebuhr's primary conviction: We cannot locate a "reason" for excessive self-regard in a psychological factor—including a lack of parental empathy. Even with all the resources available, people still chose to trust themselves rather than God, and therefore fall into sin. *This is not done merely because we feel less than human; it is also done because we want to be more than human.* Niebuhr would no doubt applaud Kohut's clinical insights into the relationship between insecurity and grandiosity. However, he would add that even very empathic parents raise children who will fall into excessive self-regard.

While we always run a risk of pushing a symbolic story beyond its explanatory insight, it is important to reiterate that for Niebuhr the Fall is not a historical or developmental "event" in our own life history. It is instead a story of ongoing temptation. Regardless of the health we've established, the financial security we've accumulated, or any other finite gain, we are always tempted to distrust God and rely on our own resources to solve the ultimate riddle of our lives. But what, again, does this mean? It means simply that there are no remedies for ontological anxiety—the anxiety of simply existing, imagining possibilities, and recognizing our limits. Life itself brings with it anxiety and this anxiety is always the breeding ground for excessive self-regard. Our anxious situation, for Niebuhr, is not psychologically conjured up; instead, it is ontologically given. To be alive is to be tempted. The story of "original sin" is not the literal turning point in humanity's cosmic history, nor is it the turning point in our own individual histories. Instead, it is a description of *the way things are*, period. In so far as we are alive and anxious, the Adam and Eve story is relevant. But once again, it is relevant not because it explains the origin of sin but because it describes our temptation in the here and now.

Kohut, Insecurity, and Irenaeus

Perhaps we could take Kohut's thought in another theological direction. We have seen that Kohut is primarily interested in the fragile and injured self beneath narcissitic posturing. Healing begins with a careful attentiveness to these underlying insecurities rather than a bold confrontation of the unwarranted grandiosity. Again, what looks like obnoxious arrogance is fueled by the pain of a shaky self. Given this, Kohut might find the perspective of Ireneaus, the most important theologian of the second century, more helpful than that of Augustine. When referring to the *imago Dei*, or divine image within each person, Irenaeus separates the words "image" and "likeness." The word "image" refers to reason, bodily powers, and freedom—qualities with which we are born. Image is automatically given; therefore there is no need to cultivate it. The word "likeness," on the other hand, refers to a gradual process by which we take on more and more of God's character. Irenaeus puts it this way:

> A mother, for example, can provide perfect food for a child, but at that point he cannot digest food which is suitable for someone older. Similarly, God himself certainly could have provided humanity with perfection from the beginning. Humanity, however, was immature and unable to lay hold of it.[37]

So while Adam was born with the image of God, he did not yet have God's likeness. Consquently, Adam was not created perfect as Augustine would later argue. The simple reason that Adam was not perfect is that he was a *created* being, and for Irenaeus, only *uncreated reality* can be perfect. Adam could not have handled perfection. Consequently, God set up a strategy whereby Adam could grow into a stronger and stronger commitment to goodness, and thereby hang on to it. From Irenaeus's perspective, Adam did not have what later Western theology would call "original righteousness." Stephen Duffy provides a good description of Irenaeus's view of the first human.

> Morally and intellectually he was a child-man not yet endowed with the Spirit of adoption. Adam, through a torturous process of growth in obedience, was meant to grow up into closer *likeness* to God. The whole sweep of history through the two testaments is to be for infanat humanity an educational process. However, due to his immaturity, Adam fell prey to a jealous Satan, disobeyed, and the process was hindered. Growth in the likeness of God, the divine strategy was retarded. This understandable, even inevitable, sin of Adam was freighted with consequences, for in him all lost what Adam lost.[38]

Irenaeus thus sees the Fall not as radical evil, but as an understandable sin. Adam, being immature, was tempted and fell. His discriminatory abili-

---

[37]Irenaeus of Lyon, "Against Heresies" in *Theological Anthropology*, ed. J. Patout Burns (Minneapolis: Fortress Press, 1981) 23.

[38]Stephen J. Duffy, *Dynamics of Grace: Perspectives in Theological Anthropology* (Collegeville MN: Michael Glazier, 1993) 47-48.

ties were not developed and he was easily misled. Irenaeus's views are in stark contrast to Augustine's portrayal of a highly punitive God who ran the once-perfect couple out of the Garden forever. For Augustine, and most of Western theology, Adam's sin has been understood as completely inexcusable.

This very old difference between Irenaeus and Augustine may seem irrelevant to a discussion of contemporary psychotherapy, but it is actually quite informative. Irenaeus seems to offer a *deficiency model* of sin whereas Augustine argues that humanity sins *out of strength* and not just deficiency. For Irenaeus, immaturity, insecurity, and ignorance are key ingredients in sin. For Augustine, the primary element is prideful rebellion. Augustine would argue that we sin with full bellies as well as empty ones; with full bank accounts as well as impoverished finances; with our needs met as well as our needs lacking. Humanity does not sin simply out of weakness; instead, we sin out of strength. Sin cannot always be traced to some form of deficiency in our lives.

It may seem to many that Irenaeus offers a more compassionate understanding of humanity's ills. Perhaps he would have made a better psychotherapist than Augustine. Again, Ireneaus believes that the fall into sin is an inevitable part of growing up and learning about life. While Augustine argues that even all natural evil is a result of sin, Irenaeus says that disasters are trials necessary for us to develop. The punishment for the first sin, according to Irenaeus, is more a sign of God's compassion than of his wrath. The experience of sin makes us appreciate God's kindness. In a sense, then, getting kicked out of the Garden was not such a bad thing. It was the path toward growing up. Sin and its consequences are our teachers. They help us appreciate God's compassion and love.

To put it psychologically, this view of the Fall is a nonshaming view. Suffering is not the horrible consequence of Adam's sin, but the vehicle of spiritual development. By concretely experiencing the differences between virtue and sin, we can *gradually* prefer goodness. But a major problem for spiritual development, according to Irenaeus, is that we do not have patience. We want too much maturity too fast. As he states it:

> People who do not wait for the period of growth, who attribute the weakness of their nature to God, are completely unreasonable. They understand neither God nor themselves; they are ungrateful and never satisfied. At the outset they refuse to be what they were made: human beings who are subject to passions. They override the law of human nature; they already want to be like God the

Creator before they even become human beings. They want to do away with all the differences between the uncreated God and created humans.[39]

Just as Kohut argues that the analyst must be empathically patient with people as they work through their narcissitic injuries and need for mirroring, so Irenaeus points toward the time-consuming task of spiritual development. It's a slow process.

Thus, Irenaeus offers a possible theological resource for those psychologies, including Kohuts's, which see insecurity, self-doubt, and a fragile self as more primary than the "grandiosity side" of narcissism. From this perspective, human beings struggle psychologically with the pains of growing up. We are often immature, self-doubting, and insecure. While we may cover these feelings with compensatory external behavior, this outward appearance does not discount our underlying anxiety.

Kohut and Grace

In the 1960s, both Thomas Oden and Don Browning made provocative and pioneering claims that psychotherapy often works within an implicit philosophical and even theological assumption about the acceptability of its clients or patients.[40] Even secular psychotherapy participates in this ontological assumption that the client/patient is acceptable before the very foundations of life. In other words, therapeutic healing goes beyond the communication that the therapist accepts the client. It also goes beyond the idea that the therapist represents the community's acceptance of the client. Instead, the therapist reflects an accepting presence which is at the very heart of reality itself. While the therapist may not realize that she is speaking as a theologian, in so far as this ontological message of acceptance is being communicated, she is. A powerful and transforming reality of grace enters the so-called secular psychotherapeutic framework even if it occurs implicitly and under the radar of conscious identification.

While Oden and Browning used the psychotherapy of Carl Rogers as their primary psychotherapeutic example, much of their argument could be applied to Kohut. Kohut seems to offer his patients an empathic, accepting

---

[39]Irenaeus, "Against Heresies," in *Theological Anthropology*, ed. Burns, 25.
[40]Thomas C. Oden, *Kerygma and Counseling* (Philadelphia: Westminster Press, 1966); Don S. Browning, *Atonement and Psychotherapy* (Philadelphia: Westminster Press, 1966).

reality which points beyond himself. He mediates, reflects, and embodies a larger sense of empathic affirmation rooted in the Source of reality. It hardly requires a stretch to see the "grace" in what he offers. He listens attentively to the self struggling beneath all the hurt, grandiosity, sense of entitlement, anger and depression. His goal is to affirm, build up, and support this wounded sense of self. He is quite ready to admit that the external appearance of this wounded self may seem obnoxiously full of itself. Yet with a stead, empathic entry into the psychological world of the patient, Kohut believes the message of hope and redemption for the injured self can be communicated. The patient is quite incapable of offering this "grace" to him or herself. The conviction of unworthiness is too strong. Once internalized, this message is too pervasive and debilitating for one to "cure" oneself. Stated more theologically, we can never offer ourselves grace. We need the acceptance of another person, an empathic understanding which can nonjudgmentally enter our internal frame of reference. We need a selfobject who reflects grace. Again, the concrete role of the Kohutian analyst is to provide this. Yet, there is a hidden assumption that life itself accepts the patient, that the ultimate selfobject (God) offers an affirmation of the struggling self. One can lay down one's guard, quit pretending, and stop resisting the reality of radical acceptance. To repeat, this is not just an anthropological assumption; it is a tacit ontological assumption about the nature of Being. The therapist does not arrive at this conviction as a result of empirical investigation or rational deduction. It is instead a philosophical premise which makes therapy possible. The therapist claims to reflect a deeper view of reality than the world of rejection and unacceptability. As Browning states it:

> In brief, the therapist's empathic acceptance announces, proclaims, and witnesses to the fact that the client is truly acceptable, not only to him as a therapist, but to some of structure which transcends all finite referents, i.e., to the universe and whatever power that holds it together. And similarly, the client does not come to feel that he is acceptable simply to the therapist, but accepts the fact that he is acceptable in an ontological sense. Without this broader context of meaning operating in the therapeutic situation, it is doubtful whether the fruit of therapy would have any generalized consequences outside the narrow confines of the therapeutic situation. Successful therapy rests upon a *generalization* of an experience the client has with the therapist. The fact that the therapist may never name this larger structure does not negate the fact that

his attitude implies it.[41]

Thus, it is quite possible that powerful encounters with this depth of acceptance in a therapist's office may also entail an encounter with Divine grace. The therapist mediates or reflects this deeper reality.

But if this accepting reality is to mean anything, it must be incarnational. Grace must come to us in flesh and blood. By that, I mean that our experiences of despair, hopelessness, and self-injury must be concretely understood. Any form of acceptance which does not enter fully into the pain of our sense of self-rejection will mean very little. Empathy is no spectator sport. While it does *not* mean feeling everything the patient feels, it *does* mean being able to understand those feelings and to stand with the person in the process. This is where detached interpretation, from Kohut's perspective, fails people. Patients must know that their hopelessness has been understood; otherwise, any suggestion of hope will seem cheap or unreal. Redemption necessitates a full tour of hell. The vague idea of our acceptability will mean little without the concrete embodiment of it. Stated another way, reading books on self-esteem in isolation will not heal the disturbance of the self. Again, this empathic acceptance must be incarnationally present.

A great deal of narcissistic posturing and attention seeking is an unfortunate attempt to gain a sense of legitimacy. To put it in more theological terms, it involves a compulsive attempt at justification. But the self we parade around others is insatiable because it does not address its own deeper needs. Even the best flattery is only temporary. Adoring attention lasts only for today. The self, when it attempts to hide its experience of injury behind exhibitionism, simply cannot get enough adoration to do the job. The frantic attempts at self-justification do not prevail. The injury does not go away. We may not realize the estrangement beneath all these attempts to win the praise of others and the narcissistic rage that issues forth when we do not receive it. Stuck in an endless cycle of audience seeking, we have no solid sense of acceptance even when others are not telling us how great we are. Grace has not been internalized. This lack of grace leads to a kind of bondage of the will in which we incessantly do the very things which will drive away the people we need. Our excessive needs for others frighten them off; and our rage at their not being there for us drives them away further. We present a self which pretends to be noninjured. Yet this pretense

---

[41]Browning, *Atonement and Psychotherapy*, 150-51.

is precisely what sabotages our possibility of healing.

What is needed is the disclosure to another of the truly fragmented, damaged, and hurting self. The posturing must stop. But this will only occur when we feel as if we are truly on the receiving end of empathic and non-judgmental attentiveness. The self-condemnation, even if hidden, is already present. As stated earlier, we cannot release ourselves from such condemnation. The doors of hell have to be opened from an empathic other.

As the patient experiences the acceptance and empathic understanding of the Kohutian analyst, he is then more open to psychological interpretation of what is occurring in his life. Again, Kohut differs from Carl Rogers in that he does *not* believe that empathy alone is enough. But interpretation is an outgrowth of empathy. No longer feeling that she is on trial, the patient can listen with new ears to an insightful interpretation. But it is because *empathy has occurred first* that interpretation is possible.

The experience of Kohutian analysis helps build and solidify the self so that self-obsession is no longer necessary. Again, for Kohut, self-obsession occurs because of untreated self-injury. We are preoccupied with ourselves because of an *insecure* rather than an overly *secure* self. A more secure self can invest in life, enjoy relationships, and continue to transform grandiosity into realistic ambitions. A more stable sense of self will involve less self-obsession. It is the fragile self which must always attend to itself and thereby miss out on much of life.

So in Kohut's framework, the self longs to be known as it is and accepted amidst all its distortions, injuries, and ugly attempts to address its needs. Narcissistic injury is not pretty. Yet it is necessary for an analyst to empathically understand this disturbed sense of self before healing can occur. Meaningful acceptance must embrace the self at its very worse. In doing this, the Kohutian analyst reflects a deeper reality of empathic acceptance which points beyond the therapy to the very Ground and Source of life. This cryptotheological function of psychotherapy may not be explicit, but it is nevertheless present.

The Kohutian analyst represents a new world to the patient—a world in which condemnation, fragmentation, or disorienting anxiety do *not* have the final word. This is a world which can be trusted, a world offering support and new possibilities. This world invites the shedding of our defenses amidst the deep sense that we are accepted. This is a world which invites us, as Paul Tillich frequently said, to "accept our acceptance." Kohut represents this world and is a "minister" in its service. The message, again, is one of grace.

Contrasting Niebuhr and Kohut

A major emphasis in Niebuhr's *Nature and Destiny of Man*, as we have seen, is the self's capacity to transcend the immediacy of its circumstances and reflect on life. In spite of social and historical necessities, we each experience a degree of freedom in that we are never completely determined by our situations. Without this capacity for self-transcendence, all "sin talk" would be meaningless. The capacity to look beyond our immediate circumstances and imagine other possibilities is the source of both creativity and moral evil. Any psychological framework which does not allow for this possibility of self-transcendence must be rejected. Kohut would certainly agree. There is, for instance, absolutely no possibility of talking about personal responsibility or sin within the paradigm of B. F. Skinner.[42] To deny the capacity for some degree of freedom—as Skinner blatantly does—is to eradicate much of what it means to be human. On the other hand, Niebuhr has a clear grasp that the self is always situated in a particular time and place and therefore subject to the limitations of these factors. In disagreeing with Skinner, he would certainly *not* embrace the radical view of human freedom in a thinker such as Sartre. We do not have an unlimited freedom. Nevertheless, we have enough freedom to trigger anxiety about the possibilities of our lives. The self is formed by its various dialogue partners and communities, but this formation is not deterministic.

By the time Niebuhr wrote *The Self and the Dramas of History* in 1955, he maintained the central theme of self-transcendence, but he portrayed the self as involved in three primary dialogues. As he put it, "The self is a creature which is in constant dialogue with itself, with its neighbors, and with God, according to the biblical viewpoint."[43] This dialogue within the self is an empirical fact in that every person can attest to this internal conversation. The self is also in ongoing conversation with others. One's sense of self is mirrored and reflected by the other. While Niebuhr does not use Kohut's technical term "selfobject," it is clear that he agrees with Kohut's emphasis on the self's need of others throughout the lifespan. And finally,

---

[42]B. F. Skinner, *Beyond Freedom and Dignity* (New York: Alfred A Knopf, 1971).

[43]Reinhold Niebuhr, *The Self and the Dramas of History* (New York: Scribner's, 1955) 4.

the self is in dialogue with God. This conversation, of course, will be much more widely disputed than the two previous ones. Niebuhr realizes this and says that this conviction is obviously beyond empirical verification. However, the idea that the self frequently *believes* it is in dialogue with God is an empirical fact. Throughout humanity's history it has longed for and believed that it was in relationship with a Source beyond itself. This yearning for the Ultimate is a definite aspect of the self's desire for relationship. Steven Wilkerson provides a very helpful overview of Niebuhr's conception of the self:

> The self is mysterious; is involved in dialogues with itself, others, and God; pities and glorifies itself; accuses and defends itself; uses conceptual images; is united but evidences different foci; discusses with itself its long and short term responsibilities; is in the total personality; possesses a will and conscience; can transcend itself conceptually and judge its goals; is radically free; experiences anxiety; possesses a universal inclination to be more concerned with itself than others; transcends its body; is engaged in a perceptual dialogue with others; uses other selves as instruments for its purposes; requires mutual love for its fulfillment; is indeterminately open to other selves; is paradoxically conditioned by historic factors and transcendent to them; is a creator of historical events; searches for ultimate meaning; finds satisfaction in a relationship with God in which it repents and opens itself to God's love.[44]

As we saw in chapter 1, Niebuhr insists that an adequate understanding of the self must acknowledge these staggering paradoxes.

Both "will" and "conscience" are manifestations of self-transcendence. Will is "the result of the self's transcendence over the complex of its impulses and desires."[45] The will represents the self's organized goals and purposes. Conscience, on the other hand, is the self's capacity to evaluate itself and to judge its activities. Conscience, therefore, represents more than social indoctrination. In fact, conscience can turn a critical eye on this indoctrination. As Niebuhr puts it, "We will define conscience, provisionally at least, as the aspect of the self's judging its actions and attitudes in which a sense of obligation in contrast to inclination is expressed."[46]

---

[44]Stephen Eugene Wilkerson, "An Analysis of the Concept of the Self in Selected Writings of Carl Rogers and Reinhold Niebuhr" (diss., Florida State University, 1980) 144-45.

[45]Niebuhr, *The Self and the Dramas of History*, 12.

[46]Niebuhr, *The Self and the Dramas of History*, 13.

Niebuhr is quite aware that efforts have been made to dismiss any serious notion of "ought," particularly by naturalistic philosophies which deny the realm of the transcendent. Yet Niebuhr points out that the self repeatedly attempts to prove that what it desires is indeed desirable and worthy of such pursuits. The self offers defenses for what it seeks, defenses which always point toward a sense of obligation to pursue higher goods. "This sense of obligation is powerful enough to allow the self freedom to achieve what it desires only when it is able to persuade itself that what it desires is consonant with the more general system of values."[47] For Niebuhr, this sense of obligation cannot be reduced to the process of socialization. Instead, it points toward the capacity for self-transcendence.

Mark Lovatt makes a helpful comparison between Niebuhr's understanding of the "will to power" and nineteenth-century philosopher Friedrich Nietzsche.[48] Nietzsche, as is widely known, argued passionately in favor of the will to power. For him, we are each a part of a world utterly riddled with chaos and meaninglessness, a world without any abiding values. Everything is constantly changing, including our own ideas about the greatest good. In such a situation we are called to aggressively forge our own sense of destiny and overwhelm our opposition. Such an energetic assertion of the will must overcome the "slave mentality" of Christianity, which Nietzsche hated. The will to power and the "death of God" in Nietzsche's thought are dual aspects of self-assertion.

Niebuhr, on the other hand, acknowledged the force of Nietzsche's will to power but understood it as more self-destructive than self-affirming. It is directly connected to human evil in that the will to power encourages excessive self-regard and a tendency to view all of reality from the standpoint of the self's own interests. As Lovatt puts it:

> To the question whether Niebuhr's use of the phrase is synonymous with Nietzsche's, the question is that it is. However, while Niebuhr's concept of the will to power correlates with Nietzsche's, his attitude towards it is diametrically opposed. While Nietzsche regards it as essential to affirm the will to power and give it free reign, at least for the overman, Niebuhr's position is that the will to power is practically the definition of human evil, and that since power corrupts, the pursuit of power by the will to power is not only to be

----

[47]Niebuhr, *The Self and the Dramas of History*, 14.
[48]Mark F. W. Lovatt, *Confronting the Will-to-Power: A Reconsideration of the Theology of Reinhold Niebuhr* (Carlisle, Cambria UK: Paternoster, 2001).

deplored, but actively resisted.[49]

For Niebuhr, as we saw in earlier chapters, the dilemma is that the self has a tendency to view its activites from the standpoint of its own interests. Part of this tendency, of course, is necessary for survival and fulfillment. Again, Niebuhr never condemns self-regard. But the self often moves beyond a healthy self-regard and places itself at the very center of life. It then spins out elaborate justifications for this undue self-focus. To repeat: For Niebuhr, this is *the central problem* of the human condition. As he put it, "The universal inclination of the self to be more concerned with itself than to be embarrassed by its undue claims may be defined as 'original sin'."[50] This breathes new life into the traditional theological concept of the "bondage of the will." Stated most directly, *the self is in bondage to itself.* This is not simply a bondage to its lower impulses. It is instead a bondage to its own self-preoccupations. Niebuhr believed that Erasmus represents the Renaissance position that the self is free over its own impulses and biological inclinations.

But for the Reformers, and particularly Luther, the bondage of the self refers to this inordinate self-focus. Endless justifications can be created when the self's own interests are at stake. And for Niebuhr, this is true of *both* the analyzed and unanalyzed self. Analysis will not get rid of this inclination toward excessive self-interest. The reason is that this undue self-focus does not result directly from pathology. Pathology may exacerbate it but it does not *cause* it. *The most analyzed self will continue to struggle with excessive self-focus.* Again, this is because even if the pre-Oedipal anxieties and injuries of selfhood are largely healed, life will inevitably serve up new dimensions of anxiety. These new forms of anxiety will tempt the self back into a preoccupation with its own security, often at the expense of others. These new anxieties will not be a simple return to pre-Oedipal issues.

Perhaps a concrete example would help. Kohut, in midlife, went through significant anxiety when he wondered if he could gain enough votes to become the president of the International Psychoanalytic Association. Was this anxiety merely a replay of his mother's empathic failures during his childhood or did it have its own roots in midlife struggles? Both

[49]Lovatt, *Confronting the Will-to Power*, 39-40.
[50]Niebuhr, *The Self and the Dramas of History*, 18.

Erik Erikson and Niebuhr would agree that this anxious experience should not be completely attributed to his pre-Oedipal relationship with his mother. As Niebuhr puts it, "This ladder of ambition and achievement is inevitably accompanied by a ladder of anxiety."[51]

Kohut also seems to imply that a healthy self will, of necessity, use selfobjects when it is vulnerable but gradually internalize those selfobject functions and establish greater self-care. This involves seeing others as truly "other" and engaging in relationships of increasing mutuality, reciprocity, and even occasional self-sacrifice. Yet Niebuhr would argue that the temptation to continue using the other as selfobjects is more persistent than Kohut acknowledges. As anxiety is faced throughout life, one is tempted to use others for one's own desired ends. Insecurity blurs others as truly "other" and instead sees them as instrumental objects for one's own self-interest. Again, this remains a lifelong temptation. While Kohut insightfully sees that in genuine love we offer ourselves as temporary selfobjects to each other, Niebuhr would perhaps suggest that Kohut minimizes the possibility of exploiting and using the other for one's own advantage.

But perhaps we should state the primary tension between Niebuhr and Kohut in its most direct way: Does the pre-Oedpial, narcissistic injury described so well by Kohut really account for Niebuhr's description of excessive self-regard in adulthood? Few would doubt that Kohut's brilliant investigation of narcissistic injury provides an excellent account of much adult narcissism. But does it really describe the entire predicament of excessive self-focus? Is narcissistic injury the primary factor behind what ails us? Or to state it differently, is there such a thing as nonpathological, excessive self-regard? Can inordinate self-concern also grow out of a "healthy" self? Does self-centeredness always arrive from some from of self-deficiency? Niebuhr does not think so:

> It also tempts psychiatry to reduce all forms of egotism to vestiges of childhood egocentricity which greater experience will correct. Thus an approach to the self which is therapeutically adequate for pathological aberrations of selfhood is incapable of comprehending the real problems of the self on either the practical or the religious level.[52]

In other words, the problem of inordinate self-regard is a *theological*

---

[51]Niebuhr, *The Self and the Dramas of History*, 21.
[52]Niebuhr, *The Self and the Dramas of History*, 11.

problem and not simply a *psychological* one. It cannot be adequately explained by an analysis of human relationships. It moves beyond what did or did not happen to us in childhood. It is an ongoing temptation regardless of our psychological health.

Niebuhr would no doubt highlight Kohut's occasional comment that he learned all he knew about narcissism from being the President of the American Psychoanalytic Association.[53] Niebuhr would be quick to point out that all these psychoanalysts had themselves been analyzed and therefore had an opportunity to greatly decrease the pathological aspects of their previous experience from childhood through the present. Yet excessive self-regard, often amidst rather impressive professional credentials, still raises its head. It is an ongoing temptation and cannot be reduced to childhood deficiencies.

Kohut would no doubt respond that the analysts to whom he referred have lingering issues of narcissistic injury which were not addressed in traditional Freudian analysis. He would perhaps say that a robust sense of self will not have a problem with inordinate self-focus. One will learn to channel earlier grandiosity into fruitful ambition. The self will be enthusiastic without being full of itself; motivated without trying to be godlike. To impose theological categories on Kohut, he seems to be saying that "sin" is an outside/in problem. In other words, destructive behavior finds its birthplace in the parents' empathic failure. Parental attitudes seem to be the "cause" of evil inclinations. All of us are fine until we are narcissistically injured. Rather than "pride coming before a fall," a self-injury is the root of our problems. While the self may appear to be exhibitionistic and grandiose, the underlying issue is woundedness. The self has not been adequately mirrored in its emotional environment and hence it craves excessive power, status, and attention.

As we have seen, Kohut suggests that later anxieties throughout the life-span resurrect the unhealed narcissistic rupture of the pre-Oedipal period. In other words, the source of later difficulties resides in the earliest stage of life. As Browning points out, this is where Kohut and fellow psychoanalyst Erik Erikson differ.[54] Erikson emphasized the anxiety associated with later

---

[53]See Charles B. Strozier, *Heinz Kohut: The Making of a Psychoanalyst* (New York: Other Press, 2001) 140.

[54]Don S. Browning and Terry D. Cooper, *Religious Thought and the Modern Psychologies*, 2nd. ed (Minneapolis: Fortress Press, 2004) 195.

transitional movements and stages of human life. Adulthood has its own forms of anxiety-producing issues and does not merely recapitulate pre-Oedipal concerns. The struggle is ongoing and each period of life pushes the individual with its on psychological crises. Even if the pre-Oedipal period was successfully handled, later issues will trigger potentially disruptive anxiety. Kohut seems to imply that if the child receives fairly committed empathic care during the early period of life, he or she will be well equipped to successfully handle later problems as well. In fact, Kohut seems close to the position of humanistic psychologists who argue that human fulfillment will naturally unfold if given the right environmental nurturing. Erikson would agree about the importance of emerging from the first stage with a strong sense of trust but this is hardly the end of the story. New challenges are ahead. Again, each new "age" of the human lifecycle has its own anxiety-provoking issues which can threaten the solidarity of the self. As Browning puts it:

> Whether it is the transition from trust versus mistrust to autonomy versus shame and doubt or the later adult transitions from generativity versus stagnation to integrity versus despair, the anxieties accompanying the subtle decisions to cope with the new circumstances of life are increasingly evident throughout the life cycle due to the pangs of freedom. Erikson could write passionately and sensitively about existential anxiety, metaphysical anxiety, and "ego chill" as he did in *Young Man Luther* (1958). He knew he was describing something that was both continuous with but certainly not exhausted by a child's fear of losing a parent or the experience of fragmentation to the elf due to a parent's unempathic responses.[55]

Perhaps a primary difference between Kohut and Niebuhr, then, can be expressed this way: For Kohut, destructive and harmful behavior emerges from the injured self, a condition traceable to pre-Oedipal issues. For Niebuhr, on the other hand, destructive and harmful behavior also emerges from the *anxiety about what might happen*. Evil can come from *anticipatory anxiety* as well as *previous injury*.

Perhaps we can put the issue this way: Both Niebuhr and Kohut agree that excessive self-focus is a major problem in our world. While some forms of self-regard or narcissism are more extensive than others, it is a universal concern. Kohut and Niebuhr are both willing to offer a universal

---

[55]Browning and Cooper, *Religious Thought and the Modern Psychologies*, 195.

description of this human dilemma. Both would also agree, at least indirectly, that the healing factor in our narcissistic self-preoccupation is grace. For Niebuhr, a preoccupation with our security is born out of a deep-rooted existential anxiety. The pretense of "mastering" our security is a mask to cover the ontological anxiety we all must face. The grandiosity pole of pride always hides its anxiety-ridden, precarious pole. Complete security, in this sense, is not our *natural* state. Our natural state is one of anxiety—not debilitating or immobilizing anxiety, but the anxiety which accompanies being creatures with infinite imaginations. No amount of therapy will take this away. It can only be continuously faced through a trust in the Source of life. This trust will never achieve a completely nonambiguous level because we will see daily reasons all around us to question this trust. But it is ultimately a confidence in the abiding trustworthiness of life in spite of what often appears to be meaningless. The ticket out of ontological anxiety is trust in God. Healing occurs as we experience the empowerment of grace and Divine love in the midst of our brokenness and frailty. Grace involves a profound validation and mirroring of the self. This Divine mirroring allows us to lay down our defensive strategies and pretentious displays of grandiosity. Grace makes the self less fragmentary and more cohesive. There is less of a need for self-focus because the essential self has been affirmed. Thus, in a sense, even for Niebuhr, inordinate self-regard is a rather painful and pitiful attempt to prove to oneself and others that the underlying feelings of shame and inadequacy are not real.

The question, however, is whether or not narcissistically inclined people (all of us!) need some confrontational help in seeing the demanding and destructive nature of our own sense of entitlement. Do narcissists sometimes need to be challenged, confronted, and even rebuked? Put more directly, is Kohut's approach too soft? Is a sense of the law necessary before grace can be appreciated? Here it would seem that Niebuhr would be closer to Kernberg's approach. Kernberg, as we saw, believed that it is not enough to offer empathic mirroring. The narcissist's underlying sense of entitlement has a hostile dimension which needs to be confronted and interpreted. Prolonged empathy may indulge this sense of self-inflation, not decrease it. Kernberg seems to have a psychological version of Luther's conviction that the proud self must be broken before grace can occur. Yet Kohut believes that we decrease the need for exhibitionistic showmanship by solidifying the actual self beneath all the posturing and *not* by confronting. In fact, confronting and challenging the exhibitionistic self will unwittingly trigger the anxieties of the insecure self and simply make the person more defensive. More energetic effort will be poured into protecting the grandiose self.

Yet as we have seen, for Niebuhr, even individuals who have a fairly solid sense of self and have dealt well with Kohut's fragmentation anxiety, will still experience an existential anxiety resulting from the experience of freedom. While Niebuhr would clearly acknowledge Kohut's interpersonal fragmentation anxiety and see it as an important finding, he would quickly add that this does not exhaust the problem of anxiety. Fragmentation anxiety may exacerbate the existential anxiety associated with our finitude and freedom, but it won't provide a full account of how to explain and cure it. It cannot be cured because it is built into life, and even with strong self-structures we'll still be tempted to focus excessively on ourselves.

5

Niebuhr and Psychology:
Concluding Thoughts

The essential homelessness of the human spirit is the ground for all religion;
for the self which stands outside itself and the world cannot find the meaning
of life in itself or the world. —Reinhold Niebuhr

It is not difficult to create a caricature of Niebuhr which seems deeply at
odds with the suggestion that he has much to offer psychology. This caricature would involve a man constantly on the run, externally focused,
uninterested in the personal dimensions of life and preoccupied with social
and political power. One might even further suggest that Niebuhr avoided
through a flurry of activities his own inner life, close relationships, and
family connections. In fact, one might even suggest that Niebuhr's robust
confrontation of excessive self-regard represents a projection of his own
struggles with ambition and fame. Perhaps he was, to borrow Jung's
language, fighting his own shadow.

Richard Fox's biography of Niebuhr created a picture not completely
unlike the above caricature. While it is beyond the scope of this book to
evaluate Fox's portrait, it is important to realize that many friends, family,
and former students of Niebuhr energetically rejected this image of the man
they had grown to love.[1] Instead, they remember Niebuhr as a man with
deep friendships, personable relationships with students, and a warm home
life. Also, the idea that Niebuhr was simply blasting away at his own
unacknowledged demons of pride does not match Niebuhr's frequent con-
fession that he, like *all* human beings, struggles with excessive self-regard
in the midst of life's anxieties. Niebuhr never denied that he was indicting
himself as well as others. Further, a Niebuhrian psychology would

---

[1]See esp. Langdon Gilkey, "*Reinhold Niebuhr: A Biography*: A Critical Review
Article." *Journal of Religion* 68 (April 1988): 263-76; Charles C. Brown, *Niebuhr
and his Age* (Harrisburg PA: Trinity Press International, 2002) 262-77.

encourage us to accept this tendency, recognize Divine forgiveness, and get on with the business of living. The last thing Niebuhr would encourage is an obsessive and morbid fixation on our excessive self-regard. That very fixation would itself continue to manifest an excessive self-regard. As we saw earlier, Niebuhr would label self-hatred as another form of self-obsession, an obsession in dire need of God's grace.

I have argued throughout this book that Niebuhr's deep understanding of the human struggle reveals a familiarity with his own psyche. Indeed, Niebuhr's masterful understanding of social and political dynamics is matched by an insightful grasp of intrapsychic dynamics. While he understood quite well the social perspectives of individuals such Hobbes and Marx, he also greatly appreciated the intrapsychic insights of thinkers such as Pascal, Kierkegaard, and Freud. Throughout his life, Niebuhr remained both a student and interpreter of anxiety.

I would like to conclude this study with a brief summary of Niebuhr's primary contributions to psychology. First, *Niebuhr offers a very important balance between individual and social concerns.* Niebuhr regularly stressed the significance of the social context of our lives and though he did not share what he called the utopian hopes of the social gospel movement, he was nevertheless constantly engaged in enhancing social justice. He internalized much of Marx, and was an irritatingly clever master at pointing out the self-interests behind so many "benevolent" social gestures. Niebuhr had an amazing grasp of world politics and resisted any view which decontextualized or dehistoricized human beings. He would no doubt agree that much of psychology has been far too individually focused, too interested in private fulfillment rather than public good.

However, Niebuhr appreciated the world of psychotherapy and under no circumstance did he reduce the human dilemma to a long series of social problems. He not only recognized the significance of individual psychopathology, but he emphasized the key role of the individual in his theological conception of sin. Because oppression is not the primary problem, human liberation should not be equated with salvation. In fact, Niebuhr argued that we sin *out of our freedom* and not *because we have freedom.* While oppression is clearly a form of sin, it is not the ultimate or only manifestation of sin. There is something deeper than oppression going on. This is why one group can escape oppression and then rather quickly begin the process of oppressing another group. Because life is fundamentally anxious and insecure, we will always be tempted to make ourselves safer and more secure than is humanly possible. This craving for greater security will inevitably spill over onto others and negatively affect their lives.

But this does not mean that Niebuhr was a defeatist. His intension was not to reinforce the status quo by telling victims that even if they gain their freedom, they'll simply do the same things their oppressors did. No, injustice must be challenged and every effort to establish a more just society must occur. Yet Niebuhr insisted on pointing out the insidious quality of excessive self-regard. While he did not want people to passively sit and do nothing about their oppression, he *did* want them to change the world with their eyes wide open. And this open-eyed stance meant *not* falling prey to the Marxist notion that "once we get in charge, everything will be wonderful." Niebuhr resisted any notion that the elimination of social evil will remedy the problem within the human heart. By this, again, he meant the problem of ontological anxiety. The mishandling of this anxiety is the primary and essential root of sin. With an awareness of this inward tendency, we can move toward a more sober view of social change, maintaining an alertness to the possibility that we may all too easily imitate yesterday's oppressors.

Mainline pastoral theology often seems to be moving dangerously close to a fixation on socioeconomic and political realties as the source of all interpersonal and intrapsychic problems. This is part of an understandable repentance from an earlier obsession with individual psychotherapy and a conviction that intrapsychic problems explain *all* human problems. But it is always dangerous when we attempt to fix yesterday's problems by moving in the opposite direction today. Courses in public policy should not replace courses dealing with psychological dynamics. There is a need to develop a double vision which takes seriously the deep wounds of a person's psyche and also recognizes the contexts in which those wounds take place. Niebuhr would support both.

Second, *Niebuhr drives every psychological perspective to be explicit about its underlying assumptions concerning human nature*. He had a remarkable ability to zero in on the assumptive world of a perspective and indicate the philosophical anthropology on which it worked. All psychological thinking is done on the basis of a cluster of assumptions about what it means to be human. Niebuhr relentlessly insisted on laying these cards on the table. As much as anything else, he was a student of human nature. He moved unhesitatingly toward the picture of the human condition ensconced in a particular perspective, and then compared it with other perspectives.

His question was always, "Which one of them best tells the human story?" Influenced by William James's pragmatism, Niebuhr was interested in the "cash value" of a theory. In other words, does a theory rise to the challenge of adequately describing the empirical world around us. Because of his temperament and cognitive orientation, Niebuhr was never interested in idle speculation. A theory of human nature must bear the fruits of explaining the world. And as we have seen, he wasn't afraid to put a theory to the empirical test. If any theory—theological, psychological, or otherwise— does not explicate human experience, then we need another theory. Theological conservatives might complain that this elevates human experience as the final criteria of theological truth. And in a sense, Niebuhr is fully committed to this aspect of liberal theology. He would point toward the myths and symbols which "tell our stories" as revelatory encounters beyond the limits of human reason, but he would nevertheless insist that revelatory symbols which do not accurately account for human experience are not valid. Niebuhr was not interested in living out of two spheres—one secular and the other sacred. Theology needs to describe the concrete, everyday world in which we live. The more lofty and unworldly it becomes, the less it will be taken seriously in a very pragmatic world. Niebuhr never changed his mind concerning the futility of passive, ongoing, metaphysical speculation. Here, as we have seen, his methodology was most different from his colleague and friend, Tillich. Yet both shared a deep concern to make explicit the underlying view of human nature with which we work.

Third, *while Niebuhr fully grasped the historical and social location of all thought, and particularly challenged any theory which claimed an Absolute status, he nevertheless believed that some perspectives are indeed much better than others.* There is a profound difference between the historical and social limitations of all thought and the relativity of all thought. The kind of extreme relativism which aften accompanies radical postmodernism ends up self-defeating. It is a nihilistic snake eating its own tail. Niebuhr would never suggest that we are so helplessly stuck in our own language game, community of discourse, or assumptive world that we can never distance ourselves from it and think critically about it. He was *not* a modernist because he believed all perspectives—even the most secular ones—begin in faith. Yet, he was *not* a postmodernist in that he thought we can think, with some success, step outside of our conceptual assumptions and critically discuss them in a public dialogue with other perspectives. Critical reason may be limited but it is valuable. As we have seen, Niebuhr was never content simply "proclaiming" the Christian message and letting the chips fall where they may. He took on the additional task of showing the relevance of this message for the paradoxes of human experience. He encouraged people to look around them and see if these seemingly "absurd" ideas didn't make sense of their world. Thus, reason is useful in seeing the relevance and empirical plausibility of the Christian faith. He would reject any position which suggests that one's faith cannot possibly make sense outside one's own conceptual community. We each participate enough in the general flow of life to point toward common human experiences. Niebuhr would oppose what postmodernists frequently call a "master narrative" *if* that narrative pretended to offer the final absolute truth about life and the human condition. However, he would not oppose such a narrative simply because it attempted to comment on something universal among human beings. For instance, all human beings have the capacity for self-transcendence, a capacity which inevitably leads them toward anxiety. This is not the condition of a particular subworld within the human community. Instead, for Niebuhr, it describes all of us.

Fourth, *Niebuhr argued persuasively that any view of human nature which does not recognize the great paradoxes of the human condition will not be adequate.* For instance, we have a thirst for honesty and a great capacity for deception; a hunger for depth and a willingness to live on the surface; a longing to love and an urge to dominate; a passion for truth and a self-serving tendency to view things only from our own interests. The heights and depths of the human condition need to be acknowledged. Any psychology which sees only darkness or negative qualities within the human condition does not adequately understand it. Yet any psychology which sees only the warm and positive dimensions of personhood, while refusing to face human destructiveness, is equally problematic. We are simply not as bad as some psychologies say we are; and we are not as good as other psychologies insist. We are profoundly ambivalent and ambiguous creatures. And again, any perspective which refuses to acknowledge this fundamental ambiguity has a one-sided view of humanity. Niebuhr had an annoying habit of pointing out how people are often not as "pure" as they claim to be; yet he also frequently pointed out that the so-called "evil ones" around us are more like us than we may comfortably think.

One of the primary ways in which the paradox of the human condition is denied is through any form of determinism. Biological determinism, whether it takes the form of Augustinian original sin or a more contemporary biochemical reductionism, destroys the capacity for human responsibility and therefore nullifies any possibility of moral accountability. As we have seen, Niebuhr did not mince words about the impossibility of the Augustinian historical-causal explanation of original sin. While the story reveals an ever-present truth, once it is taken literally and biologically it destroys the very idea of freedom which makes the concept of sin meaningful. Adam's descendants don't just sin *inevitably*; they also sin *necessarily*. This theological version of biological determinism is matched today with a psychophysiological determinism which suggests that we are in fact the puppets of our own genetic and biochemical processes. Choice is an illusion. Behavior can be completely accounted for by means of neurological investigations. Niebuhr robustly denies such determinism and argues that it fails to grasp the reality of human experience. It cannot adequately account for the human experience of choice. The same could be said of any form of external determinism which locates the "cause" of all human behavior in the environment. Surely Skinner's behaviorism moves far too easily from the lab to the full range of human experience and thereby does violence to the subjective realities of at least *some* degree of self-determination.

Fifth, *Niebuhr understands the relationship between excessive self-regard and its underlying anxiety and insecurity.* Some have suggested that Niebuhr is far too negative about the human condition in his heavy emphasis on excessive self-regard. Put more theologically, he is sin obsessed. His preoccupation with human corruption blinds him to what Abraham Lincoln frequently called the "better angels of our nature." While he claims to offer a "realistic" account of the human condition, he in fact serves up a highly negative one. While Niebuhr titled one of his early works, *Leaves from the Notebook of a Tamed Cynic*, they may well wonder if his cynicism was truly "tamed."[2]

In January 1956, Carl Rogers wrote a review of Reinhold Niebuhr's *The Self and the Dramas of History.*[3] The idea of Rogers commenting on Niebuhr was interesting in itself because at that time the two were perhaps the best known American thinkers in their respective fields. This review,

[2]Reinhold Niebuhr, *Leaves from the Notebook of a Tamed Cynic* (Chicago: Willet, Clark & Colby, 1929).

[3]Carl Rogers, "Reinhold Niebuhr's *The Self and the Dramas of History*—A Review," *Chicago Theological Seminary Register* (January 1956): 13-14.

along with extensive commentary was published two years later in *Pastoral Psychology*.[4] This discussion was no doubt one of the most provocative in the history of that journal. America's premier psychologist was blowing the whistle on America's best known theologian. And the point of contention was at the heart of each thinker's basic perspective. Rogers accused Niebuhr of misreading the human situation by arguing that humanity's primary problem is pride or excessive self-regard. This completely contradicted Rogers's deepest experiences with people in psychotherapy. Indeed, it was not excessive self-regard but low self-esteem which was the more basic problem. Rogers was quite direct:

> As I lay the book down, I find that I am impressed most of all by the awesome certainty with which Dr. Niebuhr *knows*. He knows, with incredible assurance, what is wrong with the thinking of St. Thomas Aquinas, Augustine, Hegel, Freud, Marx, Dewey, and many, many others. He also knows what are the errors of communism, existentialism, psychology, and all the social sciences. His favorite term for the formulations of others is "absurd," but such other terms as "erroneous," "blind," "naïve," "inane," and "inadequate" are also useful. It seems to me that the only individuals who come off well in the book are the Hebrew prophets, Jesus (as seen by Niebuhr), Winston Churchill, and Dr. Niebuhr himself.[5]

In short, Rogers asks whether or not Niebuhr may be guilty of the very hubris he denounces. As Rogers puts it, "I find myself offended by Dr. Niebuhr's dogmatic statements and feel ready to turn back with fresh respect to the writings of science, in which at least the *endeavor* is made to keep an open mind."[6]

Rogers *does* agree with Niebuhr's rejection of a social-scientific view which says humanity is determined by natural causes, and thus history follows a quite predictable sequence. However, Niebuhr's experience of the self is fundamentally at odds with Rogers's own experience. Though lengthy, Rogers's core critique needs to be quoted in its entirety:

---

[4]Carl Rogers, Bernard Loomer, Walter Horton, and Hans Hoffman, "Reinhold Niebuhr and Carl Rogers: A Discussion," *Pastoral Psychology* 9/85 (1958): 15-17.

[5]Carl Rogers, "Reinhold Niebuhr's *The Self and the Dramas of History*," in *Carl Rogers—Dialogues: Conversations with Martin Buber, Paul Tillich, B. F. Skinner, Gregory Bateson, Michael Polanyi, Rollo May, and Others*, ed. Howard Kirschenbaum and Valerie Henderson (Boston: Houghton Mifflin, 1989) 208.

[6]Rogers, "Reinhold Niebuhr's *The Self and the Dramas of History*," 208.

It is in his conception of the basic deficiency of the individual self that I find my experience utterly at variance. He is quite clear that the "original sin" is self-love, pretension, claiming too much, grasping after self-realization. I read such words and try to imagine the experience out of which they have grown. I have dealt with maladjusted and troubled individuals, in the intimate personal relationship of psychotherapy, for more than a quarter of a century. This has not been perhaps a group full representative of the whole community, but neither has it been unrepresentative. And, if I were to search for the central core of difficulty in people as I have come to know them, it is that in the great majority of cases they despise themselves, regard themselves as worthless and unlovable. To be sure, in some instances this is covered by pretension, and in nearly all of us these experiences are covered by some kind of façade. But I could not differ more deeply from the notion that self-love is the fundamental and pervasive "sin." Actually, it is only in the experience of a relationship in which he is loved (something very close, I believe, to the theologian's *agape*) that the individual can begin to feel a dawning respect for, acceptance of, and finally, even a fondness for himself. It is as he can thus begin to sense himself as loveable and worthwhile, in spite of his mistakes, that he can begin to realize himself and to reorganize himself and his behavior to move in the direction of becoming the more socialized self he would like to be. I believe that only if one views individuals on the most superficial or external basis are they seen as primarily the victims of self-love. When seen from the inside, this is far from being their disease. At least so it seems to me.[7]

Throughout this book, however, I have argued that while Niebuhr often painfully exposed the problem of inordinate self-concern, he clearly understood the anxiety and insecurity which generated this pretentious display. While Niebuhr is best known for his emphasis on human pride, it must also be remembered that this pride resulted from *distrust*. In other words, a trust problem precedes our pride problem. Because of Niebuhr's rigorous confrontation of self-inflated pride, it is easy to forget that a deep distrust and trembling insecurity underlies this display of arrogance. Historically, Niebuhr's time was ripe for a strong challenge to dictatorial and authoritarian political regimes. But for Niebuhr, all pride is an outgrowth of a prior distrust in our Source. Consequently, even the most self-assured displays of arrogance are in reality quite pathetic. One expands one's chest in a small pocket of time and space not realizing the enormous uncertainty, insecurity,

---

[7]Rogers, "Reinhold Niebuhr's *The Self and the Dramas of History*," 210-11.

and ambiguities of the universe. If this pride were not so destructive, it would be laughable.

As we have seen, Niebuhr believed that we human beings *really are* insecure. This is not a cognitive distortion or a misreading of life. Life is riddled with a precarious uncertainty. Without a trust in a higher reality, this anxiety is often overwhelming. Pride is a defense, an attempt to mask our "smallness" in the ultimate scheme of things. Thus, we don't simply "talk ourselves into" feeling insecure; insecurity is our true condition.

Sixth, *Niebuhr argued convincingly that human fulfillment can never be directly pursued and satisfied.* Humanity is "built" to find its ultimate purpose beyond itself rather within the narrow borders of its own happiness. Fulfillment and contentment are by-products of a larger vision which moves beyond the particular needs of the ego. As we saw, Niebuhr and Jung are in agreement here. And existential psychiatrist Victor Frankl concurs:

> Therefore man is originally characterized by his "search for meaning" rather than his "search for himself." The more one forgets oneself—giving oneself to a cause or another person—the more *human* he is. And the more one is immersed and absorbed in something or someone other than oneself the more he really becomes *himself.* . . . Once one has served a cause or is involved in loving another human being, happiness occurs by itself. The will to pleasure, however, contradicts the self-transcendent quality of the human reality. And it also defeats itself. For pleasure and happiness are by-products. Happiness must ensue. It cannot be purchased. It is the very purpose of happiness that thwarts happiness. The one makes happiness an aim, the more he misses the aim.[8]

Throughout Niebuhr's sermons, a recurring theme is this notion that the self often destroys itself because it seeks itself too narrowly. Even humanistic psychologist, Abraham Maslow, who is sometimes criticized for encouraging a narcissistic culture, argued that self-actualization always goes beyond self-esteem.[9] In his famous hierarchy of needs, the need for self-actualization comes after, and is higher than, the need for self-esteem. Contrary to popular misunderstandings, Maslow never believed that

---

[8]Victor Frankl, *The Unconscious God* (New York: Simon & Schuster, 1975) 79-85.

[9]Abraham Maslow, *Toward a Psychology of Being* (New York: Van Nostrand, 1962).

"feeling good about oneself" is the ultimate goal of life. Self-actualization inevitably takes us into a world larger than the self.

And finally, *Niebuhr offers a sobering check on all forms of utopianism which promise that human initiative, on its own, can eventually eliminate all destructiveness and evil.* For Niebuhr, the cross always symbolizes the need for Divine mercy, not the proud accomplishments of human effort. The same rigorous critiques Niebuhr applied to Marx could also be applied to psychotherapy. As Niebuhr puts it, "The conclusion most abhorrent to the modern mood is that the possibilities of evil grow with the possibilities of good, and that human history is therefore not so much a chronicle of the progressive victory of the good over evil, of cosmos over chaos, as the story of an ever-increasing cosmos creating ever-increasing possibilities of chaos."[10]

Many will continue to associate the theologian Paul Tillich far more with psychology than any other twentieth-century religious thinker. This is probably warranted. I, too, have attempted an analysis of Tillich's contribution to psychology.[11] Yet I also remain convinced that Reinhold Niebuhr has much to say to psychologists as they explore the parameters of the human condition. It is my hope that this book may help promote such a discussion.

---

[10]Reinhold Niebuhr, *An Interpretation of Christian Ethics* (repr.: San Francisco: HarperSanFrancisco, 1963; ©1935) 60.

[11]Terry D. Cooper, *Paul Tillich and Psychology: Historic and Contemporary Explorations in Theology, Psychotherapy, and Ethics* (Macon GA: Mercer University Press, 2006).

Index

acceptance
    borrowing from others, 67
    as part of psychotherapeutic approach, 106-10
accommodation, radical, 66
addiction, self-injury and, 96-99
agape
    distinct from *eros*, 58-59
    Freud perceiving as unrealistic and dangerous, 57
    transformational nature of, 57-58
    unusable as standard for social justice, 15
aggression
    externalized, 53
    passive form of, 53-54
    resulting from frustration, 92
Alcoholics Anonymous, 76
analysis
    allowing grandiosity to come forward, 88
    lack of empathy in, triggering narcissistic wound, 95
    need for, 100-101
    See also psychotherapy
anxiety
    as breeding ground for neuroses, 64-65
    becoming a problem when people distrust God, 37
    leading to excessive self-regard, 25
    destructiveness of, 28
    distrust and, 30-31
    essential to understanding human condition, 27

    existential, Beck's denial of, 31
    futility of attempting to eliminate, 72
    leading to self-avoidance, 29
    leading to trust in God, 35
    neurotic vs. ontological, 27
    ongoing dimensions of, 113, 116
    as part of human condition, 28, 35
    psychotherapy and, 34-38
    role of, 18
    self-effacing solution to, 66-69
    spiritual, 29
    See also ontological anxiety
anxiety disorders, 27
apologetic theology, 8-9
Aquinas, Thomas, 10-11
Aristotelian rationalism, 10-11
Augsburger, David, 84, 86
Augustine
    giving up on Satan, 102
    on sin, 42
    view of original sin, 54

Barth, Karl, 8, 10
Beck, Aaron, 31
behaviorism, 124
Bernstein, Richard, 7
Bingham, June, 2, 19
biological determinism, 123-24
Black, Margaret, 90-91
bondage of the will, 113
Browning, Don, 7, 22, 106
    on difference between Kohut and Erikson, 115-16
    on Freudian dualisms reaching cosmic proportions, 52-53

Fall
Augustine's view of, 105
Irenaeus's view of, 104-105
Niebuhr's approach to, 102-103
See also original sin
Feuerbach, Ludwig, 74-75
finitude, 38-39
allowing only approximation of truth, 5-6
attempting to short-circuit, 65
forgiveness, 63
Foucault, Michel, 6-7
foundationalism, 6
Fox, Richard, 12-13, 119
fragmentation anxiety, 95, 118
Frankl, Viktor, 127
freedom, denying capacity for, 110
Freud, Sigmund
believing impossible the commandment to love one's neighbor, 57
challenging Hegel, 50
describing humans' estranged existence, 43-44
differing from Niebuhr on neighbor love, 58
giving up on treating narcissists, 82-83
on humans' limited libido and love of others, 73
interrupting humanity's self-confidence, 48
Niebuhr and, 47-60
offering new vocabulary for original sin, 48-49
offering secular version of Augustine's original sin, 54
primary mistake of, 54-57
on reason being unaware of human instincts' grip on it, 49
on duality of human condition, 40
similarities of Horney's and Freud's

view of, 72
summation of Niebuhr's outlook on, 78
on war between life instinct and death instinct, 50-53
Fromm, Erich, 72-76
correlating idealization of God and debasement of humanity, 74-75
critical of Protestant reformers, 73-75
emphasizing importance of self-love in mental health, 72-73
summation of Niebuhr's outlook on, 79
utopian outlook of, 44

Gadamer, Hans-Georg, 4
Gay, Volney, 85, 95
Genesis, symbolic reading of, 42-43
Gilkey, Langdon, 4-5, 10
on four major paradoxes that Niebuhr emphasizes, 38-40
on history as nature transformed by freedom, 39-40
on human anxiety, 27
on human life transmuted by spirit, 39-40
on Niebuhr exploring human being in history, 17
on Niebuhr following Pelagius, 42
on Niebuhr addressing human nature, 20
on Niebuhr's apologetic, 22-23
on Niebuhr's individualism, 16
on Niebuhr's thought grounded in his theology, 23
on sin's effect on love and justice, 45
Glen, J. Stanley, 75-76
God
breaking through with revelatory message, 8

Niebuhr, Reinhold (*cont.*)
   viewing sin as distortion of humans'
      essential structure, 43
   view of the self, 19
   at war with oversimplification, 2
   works of, similarities with his men-
      tors, 1-2
Nietzsche, Friedrich, 6, 112-13
Nygren, Anders, 58-59

objectivity, total, fantasy of, 4
Oden, Thomas, 29, 106
Oedipus complex, 94
ontological anxiety, 27
   healing, 72
   mishandling of, 121
   no remedies for, 103
oppression, 120-21
optimal frustration, 84
optimal responsiveness, 84
Origen, envisioning final cosmic healing, 102
original righteousness, 45, 104
original sin, 42-43, 124
   Freud offering new vocabulary for,
      48-49
   Freud's secular view of, 54
   impossibility of Augustinian expla-
      nation of, 124
   See also Fall

pantheism, Niebuhr's disdain for, 36-37
parents
   offering audience for child's exhibi-
      tionism, 84-85
   self-structure of their own environ-
      ment, 87
Paris, Bernard, 71
Pascal, Blaise, on humans' true state,
   40-41
pastoral care, psychologizing and politicizing of, 18-19

pastoral psychology, moving toward
   liberationist thought, 18
pastoral theology, fixated on socioeco-
   nomics and politics, 121
Pelagius, 42
persona, recognition of, 61
philosophy, comparable to theology, 4-
   5
positive psychology, 40
postliberal theology, 12-13
postmodernism, 6-7, 99-101
predestination, psychological effect of,
   75
pride
   distrust preceding, 37
   many faces of, 33-34
   neurotic, 36
   Niebuhr's understanding of, 33-34
   related to low self-esteem, 81
   resulting from distrust, 33, 126
   underlying self-effacing solution to
      dealing with anxiety, 69
proclamation theology, 8
psychologists, indictments of own discipline, 2
psychology
   based on philosophical assumptions
      about human condition, 5
   critical hermeneutical approach to, 7
   dangerous error of, 20
   empirical, 21
   entering world of ethics, philosophy,
      and theology, 5
   humanistic, 40
   involved with physical anthropology,
      5
   moving beyond the scientific, 3
   naturalistic methodology of, 21
   Niebuhr's contributions to, 120-28
   participating in dilemma of life, 34
   popular, viewing negative thinking
      as main problem, 30-31